MARIJUANA

DATE DUE

DATE DUE

APR 3 0 2003	FEB 2 8 2006
MAY 1 1 2003	NOV 1 3 2006
NOV 1 1 2003	NOV 2 7 2006
NOV 2 5 2003	JUN 2 0 2007
DEC 0 9 2003	OCT 1 8 2007
	NOV 0 1 2007
FEB 1 8 2004	JAN 1 4 2008
APR 1 9 2004	MAR 1 9 2008
SEP 2 1 2004	DEC 1 4 2008
OCT 0 7 2004	MAY 1 6 2009
	SEP 2 3 2009
NOV 0 1 2004	OCT 1 5 2009
NOV 3 0 2004	MAR 2 2 2010
	APR 2 8 2010
MAR 2 1 2005	OCT 2 7 2010
NOV 2 8 2005	DEC 0 4 2010
	NOV 1 5 2011

MARIJUANA

by William Goodwin

DISCARD

DRUG
EDUCATION
LIBRARY

Lucent Books, San Diego, CA

*Dedicated to Donna, Gideon, Marilyn, Ashton,
Jimmy, and Meg. May your lives be blessed with love,
health, joy, peace, and kindness.*

Library of Congress Cataloging-in-Publication Data

Goodwin, William, 1943–
  Marijuana / by William Goodwin
    p.   cm. — (Drug education library)
Includes bibliographical references and index.
Summary: Discusses the history of marijuana, its
physiological and societal effects, laws regulating its
medicinal and recreational uses, and the continuing
controversy which surrounds those regulations.
  ISBN 1-56006-916-3 (hardback : alk. paper)
  1. Marijuana—Juvenile literature. [1. Marijuana.
2. Drug abuse.] I. Title. II. Series.
  HV5822 .M3 G65 2002
  362.295—dc21

                                        2001004401

Copyright © 2002 by Lucent Books, Inc.
10911 Technology Place, San Diego, CA 92127
Printed in the U.S.A.

Contents

# Foreword

The development of drugs and drug use in America is a cultural paradox. On the one hand, strong, potentially dangerous drugs provide people with relief from numerous physical and psychological ailments. Sedatives like Valium counter the effects of anxiety; steroids treat severe burns, anemia, and some forms of cancer; morphine provides quick pain relief. On the other hand, many drugs (sedatives, steroids, and morphine among them) are consistently misused or abused. Millions of Americans struggle each year with drug addictions that overpower their ability to think and act rationally. Researchers often link drug abuse to criminal activity, traffic accidents, domestic violence, and suicide.

These harmful effects seem obvious today. Newspaper articles, medical papers, and scientific studies have highlighted the myriad problems drugs and drug use can cause. Yet, there was a time when many of the drugs now known to be harmful were actually believed to be beneficial. Cocaine, for example, was once hailed as a great cure, used to treat everything from nausea and weakness to colds and asthma. Developed in Europe during the 1880s, cocaine spread quickly to the United States where manufacturers made it the primary ingredient in such everyday substances as cough medicines, lozenges, and tonics. Likewise, heroin, an opium derivative, became a popular painkiller during the late nineteenth century. Doctors and patients flocked to American drugstores to buy heroin, described as the optimal cure for even the worst coughs and chest pains.

As more people began using these drugs, though, doctors, legis-lators, and the public at large began to realize that they were more damaging than beneficial. After years of using heroin as a painkiller, for example, patients began asking their doctors for larger and stronger doses. Cocaine users reported dangerous side effects, in-cluding hallucinations and wild mood shifts. As a result, the U.S. government initiated more stringent regulation of many powerful and addictive drugs, and in some cases outlawed them entirely.

A drug's legal status is not always indicative of how dangerous it is, however. Some drugs known to have harmful effects can be pur-chased legally in the United States and elsewhere. Nicotine, a key ingredient in cigarettes, is known to be highly addictive. In an ef-fort to meet their bodies' demands for nicotine, smokers expose themselves to lung cancer, emphysema, and other life-threatening conditions. Despite these risks, nicotine is legal almost everywhere.

Other drugs that cannot be purchased or sold legally are the sub-ject of much debate regarding their effects on physical and mental health. Marijuana, sometimes described as a gateway drug that leads users to other drugs, cannot legally be used, grown, or sold in this country. However, some research suggests that marijuana is neither addictive nor a gateway drug and that it might actually ben-efit cancer and AIDS patients by reducing pain and encouraging failing appetites. Despite these findings and occasional legislative at-tempts to change the drug's status, marijuana remains illegal.

The Drug Education Library examines the paradox of drugs and drug use in America by focusing on some of the most commonly used and abused drugs or categories of drugs available today. By discussing objectively the many types of drugs, their intended pur-poses, their effects (both planned and unplanned), and the contro-versies surrounding them, the books in this series provide readers with an understanding of the complex role drugs and drug use play in American society. Informative sidebars, annotated bibliogra-phies, and organizations to contact lists highlight the text and pro-vide young readers with many opportunities for further discussion and research.

 **Introduction**

A Debate Without End

M arijuana is the subject of a great deal of debate. The only constant in the marijuana debate is disagreement. People disagree about the illegality of marijuana. They disagree about whether it is addictive. They disagree about its medical benefits. They disagree about it leading to the use of other drugs. Some argue that marijuana is a menace to society; others insist that it is not particularly harmful to individuals or society. Clearly there is very little agreement about anything regarding marijuana, and uncovering the truth is difficult.

Getting to the Heart of the Issues

After alcohol and tobacco, marijuana is the most widely consumed drug in the world, a bewildering fact in light of its almost universal illegality. In the United States, as in other parts of the world, the ongoing debate over the legalization of marijuana is often less a search for facts than a battle between people with opposing opinions. Both sides tend to make emotional arguments in support of their positions, arguments that frequently slip into unproven claims and exaggerations.

The disagreements are fueled by the lack of clear scientific understanding of the long-term effects of marijuana use, both upon individuals and upon society. Such an understanding is crucial to settling the disagreements, yet clear research results about marijuana are more difficult to obtain than for other drugs, including alcohol, tobacco, and heroin. This is because many of the effects of marijuana are extremely variable, reflecting the setting in which the drug is used and the experience of the user. There are several new research programs that are attempting to provide scientific evidence about the health and social risks of marijuana use, but until more conclusive results are obtained, the issues will remain clouded.

The controversy surrounding marijuana use today centers on several issues. First, after a decade-long decline, government statistics show that marijuana use is on the rise again among all age groups. Second, more people are rejecting the immense financial cost caused by marijuana law enforcement, eradication efforts, a judicial system overwhelmed with marijuana and other drug cases, and prisons for convicted users, sellers, growers, and importers. Third, efforts to legalize marijuana for medical purposes have gained widespread support

Activists march through Seattle, Washington, to show support for legalizing marijuana.

with new laws in favor of medical marijuana passed in Canada, several European countries, and many U.S. states. Finally, marijuana, which has traditionally been grown in less-developed countries, has become a multibillion-dollar industry in the United States, Canada, and even Switzerland. Several regions produce marijuana crops worth several times the value of all the legal crops grown in those areas.

The huge profits from this illegal marijuana industry now flow to criminal enterprises. Some studies, however, suggest that legalizing, regulating, and taxing marijuana production and sales in the same manner as tobacco and alcohol would divert these illegal profits to the government and strike a blow against drug traffickers. As with everything else about marijuana, many disagree with those studies and insist that the government has a duty to continue trying to at least reduce the amount of marijuana available to consumers with vigorous law enforcement efforts.

A lot of money is involved in the marijuana industry, both in the illegal profits and in the huge sums spent in fighting production and sale of the drug and prosecuting and imprisoning offenders. Marijuana use continues to increase along with the efforts to fight it. Patients demand the availability of medical marijuana even as opponents insist that this is just a trick to legalize marijuana. With such controversy at every turn, the marijuana debate is not likely to go away any time soon.

 **Chapter 1**

What Is Marijuana?

M arijuana has a long history in human civilization. The plants, from which the fiber hemp and the drug marijuana come, have been grown all over the world for thousands of years. Humans have found many uses for this plant, but it is its use as a drug that makes it controversial and illegal in most countries.

Marijuana Is a Drug

Drug is a medical term that describes any substance that affects the functioning of living creatures. By this broad definition many common substances contain drugs, including coffee (caffeine), beer (ethyl alcohol), cigarettes (nicotine), cough medicine (codeine and other drugs), chocolate (theobromine and caffeine), and turkey (tryptophan). The thousands of substances created and sold by pharmacological companies with the intent of treating the medical diseases and conditions of humans and animals are drugs. Hundreds of medicinal herbs used for millennia by the world's physicians to treat, cure, and prevent disease are drugs. Most of these naturally occurring drugs, however, have been replaced with synthetic pharmaceutical drugs, which are usually more effective and more profitable than herbs.

In addition to the drugs used for medical treatment, many legal and illegal drugs are used to create feelings of pleasure, excitement,

Marijuana plants are the source of hemp fibers, used for various products beyond the controversial drug.

sleepiness, sleeplessness, and other sensations. Such drugs that affect the mind or behavior of the user are often termed psychotropic, which means the drug moves toward the mind rather than other parts of the body. This group includes marijuana as well as ethyl alcohol, nicotine, heroin, cocaine, methamphetamines, hallucinogens, and many other substances.

Although most drugs have legitimate medical purposes, many people use psychotropic drugs to get "high," which means to feel one or more nonmedical drug effects like pleasure, excitement, sleepiness, and sleeplessness. In addition, many people also use drugs that have genuine medical value for getting high. Excessive or nonmedical use of drugs is often described as drug abuse.

Drugs that have medical value are listed in a special type of catalog called a pharmacopoeia. Marijuana has been considered a medicinal drug throughout most of human history and has been listed in most pharmacopoeias until recently. In fact, the oldest known pharmacopoeia, a nearly four-thousand-year-old stone tablet from ancient Babylon, lists marijuana. Almost as old, a Chinese book on medical drugs called the *Shen-nung Pen-tshao Ching* describes marijuana's ability to reduce the pain of rheumatism and certain digestive disorders. Marijuana was listed in the United States Pharmacopoeia until 1941, when it was removed following the passage of the Marihuana Tax Act, which prohibited doctors from prescribing it.

Dangerous Drugs

Drugs cause a great variety of effects in humans and animals. Some of the effects can make drugs difficult or dangerous to use even when they have medically important properties. Two of these effects are called dependence and tolerance. These effects make drugs like morphine, a troublesome medication that requires careful management by a physician, one of the strongest painkillers known to medicine.

Dependence means that a person's body chemistry responds to a drug by developing the need to continue taking it to avoid unpleasant, painful, or even deadly reactions; in addition to whatever else a dependence-causing drug does (for example, kill pain, relieve fever, make a person high), it also produces extremely undesirable effects when the person tries to stop using it. These effects, called withdrawal symptoms, include breathing difficulty, muscle and joint pain, headaches, irritability, nausea, sweating, hallucinations, sleeplessness, psychosis, and, in the worst cases, death. When a drug causes severe dependence, meaning that the withdrawal symptoms themselves are severe, it is said to be addictive. Two of the most powerfully addictive drugs are nicotine, found in tobacco products, and opiates, found in heroin and morphine. Whether or not marijuana is addictive is a matter of disagreement, but it does cause mild withdrawal symptoms in a small percentage of users.

The likelihood of developing dependence increases if a drug causes tolerance. Tolerance describes the need to take ever-increasing amounts of the drug to obtain the same effect that a small dose once provided. As users begin taking such a drug more often, larger quantities of the drug are needed to achieve the same effect and to avoid unpleasant withdrawal symptoms. In most cases a drug that causes dependence, tolerance, and withdrawal is considered unsafe for human use.

The federal government's Food and Drug Administration (FDA) has the job of approving the safety of food and drugs. Drugs that the FDA determines to have little or no medical value and a high likelihood of being abused—not always with full agreement from the medical and scientific experts—are generally illegal to use, buy, or sell under any circumstances except for rigidly controlled research purposes. Some drugs currently judged by the FDA to have no medical value include heroin, lysergic acid diethylamide (LSD), and, since 1937, marijuana.

Source and Appearance of Marijuana

Marijuana comes from the flowering tops and leaves of two closely related species of plants known by the scientific names Cannabis sativa and Cannabis indica. Both species also produce the fiber known as hemp that is used for rope and fabric. In fact, the marijuana plant itself is often called hemp because its fiber has been so important throughout history.

With such a long history of cultivation, many varieties of cannabis plants have developed so that today cannabis is grown in almost all climates. All it needs is lots of sunshine, soil, and water; so besides intentional cultivation, it sometimes also grows wild. Law enforcement agencies have discovered wild and cultivated marijuana growing in places as diverse as Alaska, Hawaii, Switzerland, Brazil, and Africa.

Marijuana is usually a green, brown, or gray mixture of dried leaves, stems, flowers, and seeds from the cannabis plant. Marijuana might come as a crumbly brown mixture of dried material resembling the common kitchen spice oregano. Or it can appear as a pressed mass of light green vegetable matter. In its dry form, it can have a very strong fragrance, often musty or spicy, or almost no smell at all.

Hashish, often called simply hash, is a form of marijuana that is popular in Europe and Asia. It is an aromatic, solid material made by collecting the resin droplets that coat the leaves and flowers of mature cannabis plants and pressing them into patties of hashish. One of the most potent forms of cannabis is a thick green or black oil,

Marijuana is derived from the flowering tops of Cannabis sativa and Cannabis indica plants.

known as marijuana oil or hash oil, that is made by cooking marijuana or hashish in alcohol to concentrate the active ingredient.

Different Names and Forms

With a long history of cultivation by many different civilizations, it comes as no surprise that there are a great number of words for marijuana (sometimes spelled *marihuana*). *Marijuana*, a Spanish word, is one of the most common names for the drug, but many people in medicine and research now refer to marijuana as cannabis (KAN-nah-biss), which is part of the scientific name for the plant from which marijuana is derived. The term *cannabis* is also used increasingly by journalists in newspaper and magazine articles in place of *marijuana*.

Although *cannabis* is now the name preferred by many scientists, political leaders, and medical professionals, there is a large vocabulary of popular-slang, and underground terms for marijuana. Some of the more common terms for this drug in the United States include *pot, dope, weed, herb, grass, bud, Mary Jane, reefer, hydro* (refers to marijuana grown in nutrient-rich water without soil), *pakalolo* (Hawaii), and *smoke*. Terms from other cultures for marijuana include *hashish* (Asia), *ganja* (India, Caribbean), *kif* (Morocco), *sinsemilla* (Latin America), *mota* (Mexico), *dagga* (South Africa), *bhang* (India), and *macoinha* (Brazil).

Hemp, Marijuana's "Good" Side

Cannabis plants have been grown for hemp fiber for thousands of years. Hemp was grown in all of the American colonies before and after independence and formed a valuable raw material throughout American history until the end of World War II. The varieties of cannabis plants used for fiber contain only small amounts of the psychotropic ingredients found in the varieties that produce marijuana.

Even though industrial hemp is illegal to grow in the United States today, in 1994 the American Farm Bureau Federation described it as a strong and versatile agricultural crop cultivated in many other countries. Currently, hemp is grown legally throughout much of Europe and Asia, and Australia and Canada are both considering legalizing industrial hemp farming. In France, for instance, where approximately ten thousand tons of industrial hemp are harvested annually, bales of hemp hay coated with cement are used to restore and build houses and walls. Various parts of the plant can also be used to make textiles, paper, paints, clothing, plastics, cosmetics, foodstuffs, insulation, and animal feed. Hemp produces a higher yield of fiber per acre than cotton and other fiber-producing plants. In addition, hemp has an average growing cycle of only a hundred days, and after harvest the soil is left virtually weed-free for the next planting.

The Chemistry and Action of Marijuana

The components of marijuana that create both the drug's high and its medicinal effects belong to a family of chemicals called cannabinoids. Marijuana contains more than sixty different cannabinoids, all found only in the cannabis plant. Furthermore, when marijuana is heated or burned, chemical changes occur that increase the number of cannabinoids and their derivatives. The resulting large number of chemicals interact in complex ways. This is one of the reasons marijuana is so difficult to study.

The most psychotropic of the cannabinoids is the compound delta-9-tetrahydrocannabinol, usually shortened to THC. Dried marijuana may contain anywhere from 2 to 20 percent THC, with the average being 4.2 percent.

Until banned in the United States during World War II, hemp was a valuable raw material used to make clothing, such as this dress.

What Purpose Does THC Serve in the Plant?

The fact that THC produces an effect on the human brain is an accidental outcome of a complex chemistry that serves other purposes for the plant. Scientists are still researching the value of cannabinoids to the plant, but it appears certain that these substances are important to the plant's survival. Because of the complex structure of the cannabinoid compounds and the resin glands that produce them, scientists do not believe that THC and other cannabinoids are merely by-products or waste products of the plant's metabolism. Instead, cannabinoids appear to be used by the plant for a number of purposes, most having to do with protecting the plant from predators and helping it reproduce successfully.

Most scientists now believe that the primary purpose of these complex and biologically active compounds is to protect the plant from other organisms. The fragrance and taste of the cannabinoids that coat the leaves and flowers seem to discourage insects and plant-eating animals from consuming the cannabis plants before they have produced seeds.

Cannabinoids also appear to play another important role in the plant's biological success. Scientists have found evidence that cannabinoids released into the soil help the plant compete for growing room by chemically discouraging the seeds of other species from germinating too close to a cannabis plant. The sticky nature of cannabinoid resins may also help pollen grains from male plants adhere to the flowering parts of the female plants.

The amount of THC in marijuana determines its potency as a drug. The leaves of industrial hemp cannabis have very low THC content (less than 1 percent of the dry weight) while the flowering tips of mature female marijuana plants have a higher concentration of THC (varying between 2 percent and 20 percent of the dry weight).

When THC is consumed, either by smoking or ingesting marijuana, the human body reacts in a number of ways. Peak levels of THC in the blood usually occur within ten minutes of smoking marijuana, and intoxication lasts approximately two to three hours. Because it dissolves poorly in water and very well in fat (lipids), THC and other cannabinoids accumulate in the body's fatty tissues, including the brain and testes. Since cannabinoids and their breakdown product, called metabolites, linger in these tissues for weeks and sometimes even months, drug tests can appear positive for cannabinoid compounds for a long time after using marijuana.

Scientific research during the 1990s made great strides in understanding how THC and other cannabinoids act in the human body. One of the most important findings of this research was the discovery that the brain and other parts of the body contain cannabinoid receptor sites, places where cannabinoids can change the chemistry of that region. (Researchers also found natural cannabinoids in the human body, which explains why the body has cannabinoid receptor sites in the first place.)

In the part of the human brain known as the hippocampus, scientists found large numbers of cannabinoid receptors. It is here they believe THC produces the marijuana high. When THC attaches to the abundant cannabinoid receptors found in the hippocampus, it causes the brain to suffer a partial loss of short-term memory. The hippocampus interacts with other brain regions to transfer new information, like a math lesson or friend's phone number, from short-term memory into long-term memory. Consequently, new information may never register in long-term memory while the brain is under the influence of marijuana.

Marijuana's effects are not limited to the hippocampus, however. Besides making a person high and interfering with memory, marijuana can cause some people to experience uncontrollable laughter one minute and paranoia the next. These effects are due to cannabinoid receptors in another part of the brain, the limbic system, where emotions are produced.

How Is Marijuana Consumed?

To produce its effects, molecules of marijuana's active ingredients (especially the THC) need to reach the brain through the bloodstream. This is accomplished by smoking or ingesting (eating or drinking) marijuana.

Marijuana is smoked far more often than it is eaten, however. The primary reason for this is that smoking produces the high almost immediately while eating it takes anywhere from thirty minutes to an hour. Marijuana is typically smoked in a hand-rolled cigarette called a joint or in any of a variety of pipes. A type of pipe that delivers a particularly large amount of smoke during each inhalation is called a bong.

Another reason smoking marijuana is more widely practiced than eating it is that smoking allows for more precise dose control. When the drug is smoked, users can tell almost at once if they have taken in enough for the desired effect. With eating, it can be an hour before users can tell if they have too much or too little THC in their bloodstream.

Effects of Marijuana

Consuming marijuana causes a number of effects on the user. In a social setting, marijuana may cause infectious laughter and talkativeness. In addition, short-term memory, attention, coordination, and reaction time are impaired while a person is under the influence of marijuana. Soon after smoking marijuana, a user also usually has bloodshot

Marijuana is most often smoked in either a pipe, or bong (left), or hand-rolled into cigarettes, called joints.

eyes and a dry mouth. And, within a few hours of smoking marijuana, most users become sleepy.

The total set of effects, however, varies from person to person. Further, the same person can experience different effects depending on how strong the marijuana is, his or her mood while using it, where the drug is used, and whether or not other drugs (including alcohol) are being used at the same time.

The most commonly reported unpleasant side effects of occasional marijuana use are anxiety and panic. These effects are reported more often by inexperienced users, and these unpleasant feelings are often the reason new users stop taking the drug. More experienced users also have reported feelings of anxiety and panic after receiving a much larger than usual dose of THC.

One reason marijuana causes anxiety is that it can increase the user's heart rate by 20 to 50 percent within about ten minutes of smoking it and about half an hour of eating it. This elevated heart rate, which can continue for as long as three hours, may be accompanied by a slight increase in blood pressure while the user is sitting and a slight decrease when standing. The light-headedness that can result from this may also intensify the user's feeling of anxiety. Despite this group of effects, cannabinoids are not considered especially toxic and there are no confirmed reports worldwide of human deaths from cannabis poisoning.

Nevertheless, marijuana, like tobacco and alcohol, has the potential to cause permanent harm to children if used by their mothers during pregnancy. Although there is considerable disagreement among scientists and doctors as to the severity of the problem, there is evidence that low birth weight and physical abnormalities have occurred among babies whose mothers used the drug during pregnancy.

There is stronger evidence that marijuana use has a negative impact on athletic performance, a result of research showing impairments in coordination, reaction time, and concentration caused by marijuana. Furthermore, some studies have found that athletic performance might be impaired for as long as twenty-four hours after marijuana use.

Marijuana's Effect on the Heart and Lungs

The increased heart rate associated with marijuana use can cause other problems. A 1999 report on medical marijuana from the U.S. government's Institute of Medicine (IOM) noted that even though the elevated heart rate experienced by marijuana users is not considered excessive for people in good health, among those with heart disease, such a rise in heart rate could be fatal.

In such cases, marijuana smokers with unidentified heart disease may be vulnerable, especially during the first hour after smoking, to an increased risk of heart attack. In a 2000 report from the American Heart Association (AHA), researchers questioned 3,882 middle-aged and elderly patients who had suffered heart attacks. Of that group, 124 admitted to being current marijuana users, 37 had used the drug in the twenty-four hours preceding their heart attacks, and 9 had used it in the hour before. The AHA pointed out that this was the first time science had found evidence that marijuana might trigger a heart attack in susceptible individuals. The report concluded that among this age group the risk of having a heart attack during the first hour after smoking marijuana is five times greater than it is in people who never use the drug.

The AHA report also stated that the cardiac risks from marijuana appear to be much lower than those from cocaine, which causes a much sharper rise in both heart rate and blood pressure than marijuana. The overall public health threat from marijuana, however, could be even greater because marijuana use is more widespread than cocaine use.

Other studies conducted by government and other research facilities contend that the only proven long-term effects of marijuana use are all related to risks posed by smoking. Users usually inhale marijuana smoke deeply and hold the smoke in their lungs for at least several seconds. Marijuana smoke contains tar, carbon monoxide, and many complex chemicals, almost all of which are respiratory irritants and potential cancer-causing agents. In fact, according to the IOM report, each inhalation of marijuana smoke contains three to five times more tar and carbon monoxide than an equal amount of tobacco smoke. Therefore, a person who smokes marijuana daily for years might face the same respiratory problems as a tobacco smoker. These individuals may cough more often, produce more phlegm, show symptoms of chronic bronchitis, and have more frequent chest colds. Long-term smoking of marijuana can also damage lung tissues and make breathing difficult. The reason marijuana smokers do not

Who Smokes Pot?

Many people have stereotypical views of who uses marijuana. Some people want to change the image of marijuana users. In the June 28, 2001, issue of *NORML News,* an article entitled "We're Your Good Neighbors. We Smoke Pot" provides some examples of ordinary citizens "coming out" about their marijuana use.

Near Portland, Oregon, a June 2001 full-page advertisement in the *Willamette Week* newspaper had folks scratching their heads. At the top of the advertisement was the headline "We're Jeff and Tracy. We're your good neighbors. We smoke pot."

Jeff Jarvis and Tracy Johnson, the Oregon couple who ran the advertisement, are calling on mainstream Americans to come out of the closet regarding their use of marijuana and show people that marijuana smokers are not a threat to society. Their ad read, "The United States government acknowledges that over 70 million American adults have smoked pot. That's one in three of your neighborhood doctors, grocers, college professors, police officers, computer programmers, postal carriers, engineers, business executives, and spiritual leaders. These pot smokers are your elected officials. They are your dearest friends. They are your family members."

The Oregon couple are part of a growing movement to "come out of the closet" about marijuana use. Mara Leveritt, senior editor for the *Arkansas Times,* took this movement one step further by publicly admitting her use of marijuana in an op-ed column that appeared in her newspaper in the spring of 1995. She wrote:

> For the past two decades, I have smoked, on average, about a joint a day. . . . If long-term, regular users like myself felt free to articulate their experiences with marijuana, the walking, talking evidence we'd represent could put our marijuana laws to shame. We may not all be intellectual and moral paragons [models]. . . . On the other hand, few of us are wild-eyed marauders, genetic mutants, or drooling derelicts from whom society need protect itself. And as we get older, our lives begin to make the lies that have been broadcast about marijuana look even more ridiculous.

Leveritt and the couple from Oregon join many other marijuana advocates who want people to know that most cannabis users are responsible citizens. According to them, Americans don't have to be afraid that marijuana use is going to spread throughout society—because it already has.

commonly exhibit such health problems, according to the IOM report, is that they usually smoke much less than tobacco smokers.

Although many people consider marijuana to be a dangerous
drug, and many studies confirm that users do indeed place themselves at risk for health problems, the extent of those problems and
how much of a risk they pose remain controversial. Now a wave of
new research is showing that marijuana is neither as dangerous to society and individuals as some previously believed or as entirely harmless as others have believed.

 **Chapter 2**

Is Marijuana Use Really Harmful?

Not everyone agrees that there is such a thing as a "marijuana culture," but when the term is used in the news, it generally refers to a group of people who are marijuana users and who, by their style of dress, music, symbols, and values, intentionally set themselves apart from mainstream society. These marijuana users tend to view people who are anti-marijuana but use alcohol and tobacco as hypocrites. Opponents of this "marijuana culture," on the other hand, feel that since marijuana users do not respect the marijuana laws and encourage other people to use the drug, they are a threat to law-abiding society.

Although the existence of a "marijuana culture" is questionable, the growing number of marijuana users in society is evidence that the popularity of this drug is increasing. It is, therefore, important to determine just how widespread marijuana use truly is, in what ways it is harmful, how serious these threats are, and how they rank compared to alcohol, tobacco, and other illegal drugs. Further, it is important to identify how society acquires its views of marijuana users and how accurate those views are.

How Common Is Marijuana Use?
According to a 1998 federal government survey, marijuana is the most commonly used illegal drug in the United States. This survey

found that there were about 2.1 million people who started using marijuana in 1998, and that more than 72 million Americans twelve years of age and older (33 percent of that population) had tried marijuana at least once in their lifetimes. When those numbers are compared to a 1985 survey by the same organization, it is clear that marijuana use is increasing. The 1985 survey found 56.5 million Americans twelve years of age and older (29.4 percent versus 33 percent in 1998) had tried marijuana at least once in their lifetimes. Further, according to the National Institute on Drug Abuse (NIDA), use among high school–aged people alone increased by about 56 percent between 1991 and 1998.

Another indication that marijuana use is on the rise in the United States is the amount of money spent on the drug. Various government agencies report that Americans spend between $7 billion and $11 billion on marijuana each year, and those agencies report that these figures may be low.

Marijuana use is clearly very common, and use is increasing across all social, age, and ethnic groups. During the early part of the twenti-

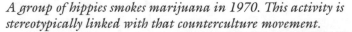

A group of hippies smokes marijuana in 1970. This activity is stereotypically linked with that counterculture movement.

eth century, for instance, marijuana use in the United States was largely confined to African Americans and immigrants from Mexico, but by the 1970s and continuing into the present, surveys and arrest records show that marijuana users now represent the entire spectrum of American society.

Marijuana in Movies and Music

One of the most common ways that ideas, including ideas about marijuana, spread throughout modern society is by popular entertainment, especially movies and music. Until recently, no far-reaching analysis of how drugs are portrayed in the popular media existed. In 1999, however, the White House Office of National Drug Control Policy (ONDCP) released the first study designed to measure the frequency and nature of illegal drug, alcohol, and tobacco use in popular movies and music. This study determined how often illegal drugs, alcohol, and tobacco were mentioned or shown in movies and music as a first step toward understanding the possible connection between media representations of substances and real-world substance use. The researchers found that an extremely high percentage of the movies studied (98 percent of the two hundred most popular movie rentals of 1996 and 1997) showed tobacco, alcohol, or illegal drugs being consumed. Tobacco and alcohol appeared in more than 90 percent of the movies, and illegal drugs appeared in 22 percent of the movies. Further, one-fourth of the movies depicting illegal drugs contained graphic portrayals of drug preparation and consumption.

Researchers also looked at the thousand most popular songs of 1996 and 1997 and found that more than a quarter of them contained clear references to either alcohol or illegal drugs, although only 2 percent of the songs had substance use as a central theme. Only about a fifth of these songs mentioned any consequences of drug use, being arrested or getting addicted, for example. Use of illegal drugs was associated with wealth or luxury in a fifth of the songs in which drugs appeared, with sexual activity in about a third, and crime or violence in a fifth. The researchers also found that references to drug use were far more common in rap music (63 percent of all rap songs) than any other type of music, including alternative rock

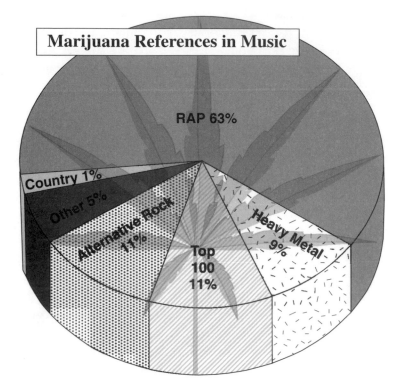

Marijuana References in Music

RAP 63%

Country 1%

Other 5%

Alternative Rock 11%

Top 100 11%

Heavy Metal 9%

(11 percent), top 100 (11 percent), heavy metal (9 percent), or country-western (1 percent).

Although no statistics prove that drug messages in movies and music actually cause drug use, there is a general feeling among many people that the media help shape society's ideas of what is normal and acceptable. If there is such a thing as a "marijuana culture," say the critics, the creators of popular entertainment must accept a good deal of responsibility for creating and spreading it.

Marijuana on the Internet

Marijuana is also consistently one of the top one hundred words looked up on the Internet's search engines. It is possible to find pictures of marijuana, learn how to grow it, find out how to beat a drug test, become a connoisseur of different types of marijuana, chat with other users about their marijuana experiences, buy drug paraphernalia, and even purchase marijuana seeds.

Marijuana Internet sites are about equally divided between those presenting a wide range of information about the drug and those offering marijuana-related merchandise for sale. From smoking paraphernalia to pro-pot T-shirts, marijuana-related products are abundantly available on the Internet. Exact figures on how much money is spent via the Internet on products related to marijuana and other drugs are difficult to determine, but the sites advertising this merchandise number in the thousands.

This particular branch of e-commerce disturbs many people, particularly because so many teens are attracted to it. Statistics show that teenagers spend more time online than any other age group, and the operators of the unregulated marijuana websites appear to recognize this fact. Critics argue that many of the sites direct much of their advertising, by language and images, at kids and teens.

Looking at the prevalence of marijuana-related items and information on the Internet and in other media, many people conclude that there is an organized, highly visible, and active pro-marijuana culture in America. Pro-marijuana messages show up in popular mainstream movies (*Saving Grace, Cheech and Chong's Up in Smoke*

Movies like Cheech and Chong's Up in Smoke *offer pro-marijuana messages to mainstream audiences.*

series, *Half-Baked,* and *Stepmom,* to name a few), music, magazines, books, political rhetoric, and television shows (for example, *That '70s Show*). As a result, several organizations, including the National Institute on Drug Abuse and U.S. Department of Health and Human Services, have begun programs that address this imbalance between pro- and anti-marijuana messages in the popular media to prevent further encouraging youth to embrace marijuana culture.

A "Gateway" Drug?

One of the most common reasons opponents of marijuana view the drug as harmful is that they believe it leads to the use of "harder" drugs such as heroin, LSD, and cocaine. Indeed, numerous studies have found that most users of heroin, LSD, and cocaine used marijuana before they used the more harmful substances. Those studies, however, also found that most marijuana users never go on to use other illegal drugs.

In fact, a large body of statistical evidence actually supports the view that marijuana does not typically function as a gateway drug. As marijuana use in the United States increased during the 1960s and '70s, use of heroin, a strong and very addictive drug, declined. Then when marijuana use declined during the 1980s, heroin use remained fairly stable. In addition, from 1960 to 1990, as the percentage of the American population using marijuana went up and down, the percentage of the population using the drug LSD hardly changed at all. Likewise, cocaine use increased in the early 1980s as marijuana use was declining. And during the 1990s, cocaine use continued to decline as marijuana use increased slightly.

According to the Lindesmith Center–Drug Policy Foundation, of all the high school seniors in 1994 who had ever tried marijuana, less than 16 percent had ever tried cocaine, the drug most often associated with the alleged gateway effect of marijuana. In fact, the proportion of marijuana users trying cocaine has declined steadily since 1986. The Lindesmith Center found no studies whatsoever that linked marijuana use with an increased likelihood of using harder drugs like cocaine and heroin.

In short, numerous researchers have found no evidence that marijuana use inevitably leads to the use of other drugs. The 1999 U.S.

government IOM report on medical uses of marijuana states, "There is no conclusive evidence that the drug effects of marijuana are causally linked to the subsequent abuse of other illicit drugs." [1]

This is the case in other countries, too. In the Netherlands, for example, where marijuana use among young people increased during the 1990s, cocaine use decreased and remains considerably lower than in the United States. In the Netherlands, marijuana is legal if purchased in government-regulated outlets, a policy designed specifically to separate young marijuana users from the illegal markets where heroin and cocaine are sold. The Netherlands was the first country to enact legislation based on the notion that marijuana users would not even be exposed to drugs like cocaine and heroin if marijuana use were legalized, and the Dutch government considers this policy successful in reducing hard drug use.

American proponents of marijuana legalization, like the National Organization for the Reform of Marijuana Laws (NORML), agree with the conclusions of the IOM report and the marijuana policy of the Netherlands. NORML asserts that the real gateway effect of marijuana use is not the result of any tendency of marijuana to make users crave stronger drugs but its illegal status, which exposes buyers to more dangerous drugs on the black market. As long as marijuana is illegal, NORML and others say, users are more likely to be exposed to heroin and cocaine when buying marijuana from illegal sources, because those people are sometimes the same dealers who sell more dangerous, addictive drugs.

Does Marijuana Use Cause Dependence or Addiction?

Most scientific medical evidence indicates that marijuana is not addictive in the way that heroin, nicotine, and other drugs are addictive. Marijuana generally does not make a user's body so dependent on the drug that the person feels physically compelled to keep using it. Nevertheless, all drugs can be used in an addictive fashion by some people, and that includes marijuana. This possibility is another reason marijuana opponents contend that the drug is harmful.

For a drug to be classified as addictive, there needs to be evidence that using it causes substantial numbers of users to fail repeatedly in their attempts to stop using it. Heroin and nicotine, for instance, meet this definition, and both are considered highly addictive. Based on numerous national studies, however, marijuana does not appear to meet this definition of addictiveness.

This is because the great majority of people who have used marijuana do not become regular users. For example, a 1993 report by the Lindesmith Center found that about 34 percent of Americans had used marijuana sometime in their life, but only 9 percent had used it in the past year, 4.3 percent in the past month, and 2.8 percent in the past week. The report also described a study of young

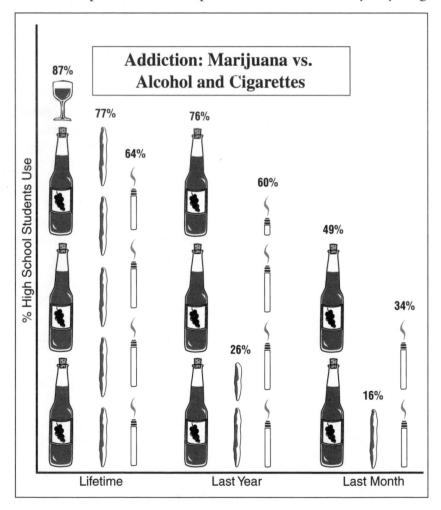

adults who had first been surveyed in high school. The study found that even though many students had tried marijuana, most had not continued using it: 77 percent reported they had used the drug—but 74 percent of those had not used it in the past year, and 84 percent had not used it in the past month.

In addition to the Lindesmith Center study, many other private and government research studies have sought to determine if marijuana actually does produce the classic symptoms of addiction in humans, including physical dependence, tolerance, and withdrawal. In 1972 during the Nixon administration, growing marijuana use prompted the federal government to review the existing studies on the drug. After studying all the available information, the government issued a report concluding that marijuana does not possess physically addictive traits. Since then the vast majority of articles published in medical journals have agreed. Two reports in particular—one from the Addiction Research Center (part of the National Institute on Drug Abuse) and another from the University of California—compared the addictiveness of heroin, cocaine, nicotine, alcohol, caffeine, and marijuana. These reports found nicotine to be the most addictive and marijuana the least addictive of the drugs studied. Marijuana also ranked last in terms of producing a physical tolerance to the drug and was deemed least likely to produce signs of withdrawal upon quitting. According to the 1999 IOM report on marijuana's potential medical uses, "Compared to most other drugs . . . dependence among marijuana users is relatively rare. . . . [T]he proportion of marijuana users that ever become dependent is 9 percent of all users, compared to 32 percent of all tobacco users, 15 percent of all alcohol users, 17 percent of all cocaine users, and 23 percent of all heroin users."[2]

Even so, some researchers contend that there is evidence to show that some marijuana users experience some withdrawal symptoms when they want to stop using the drug. These symptoms are minor, however, when compared to the withdrawal symptoms experienced by users of highly addictive drugs like heroin or nicotine. In the words of the 1999 IOM report, "Although few marijuana users develop dependence, some do. . . . A distinctive marijuana withdrawal

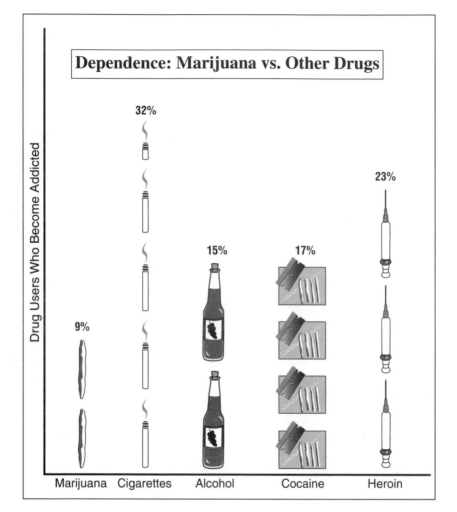

Dependence: Marijuana vs. Other Drugs

Drug Users Who Become Addicted

Marijuana 9%

Cigarettes 32%

Alcohol 15%

Cocaine 17%

Heroin 23%

syndrome has been identified, but it is mild and short-lived. The syndrome includes restlessness, irritability, mild agitation, insomnia, sleep disturbance, nausea, and cramping."[3]

Another fact marijuana opponents point to as an indication that marijuana may be addictive after all is the rise in recent years of marijuana addiction treatment programs. At first glance, this would seem to confirm the existence of marijuana addicts, but on closer examination, even this situation is ambiguous. Corresponding to the increase in treatment programs, there has been an increase in drug testing in the workplace, schools, and elsewhere. When an employee fails a drug test by testing positive for marijuana, that person is usually given the option of going to a treatment program, getting fired from the job, or being arrested. Marijuana supporters contend that this choice of options has given rise to an increase in the number of people voluntarily entering treatment programs for marijuana dependence. Neither side yet has unambiguous evidence to support its position.

Does Marijuana Cause Lung Disease?

Marijuana may not be as addictive as some other drugs, but marijuana smoke does contain lung irritants that could increase the risk of lung disease. Although frequent marijuana smokers report respiratory problems like chronic cough, phlegm, and wheezing, clinical studies of daily marijuana users have found no increased risk of serious lung diseases like chronic bronchitis, emphysema, or lung cancer.

In one study, conducted continuously since 1982 at the University of California, Los Angeles, (UCLA) Medical School, researchers have compared marijuana-only smokers, tobacco-only smokers, smokers of both, and nonsmokers. They found that some marijuana-only smokers developed lung problems, but such problems were much less frequent and less pronounced than those found in tobacco smokers. In addition, the impairments found in marijuana-only smokers occurred primarily in the lung's large airways, not the smaller, more delicate airways. Since repeated inflammation of the small airways leads to chronic bronchitis and emphysema, marijuana smokers, the study concluded, are not likely to develop these diseases.

Marijuana is usually smoked unfiltered, which allows more of the tar and other substances found in burning vegetable matter into the user's lungs. Furthermore, because most marijuana smokers inhale deeply and hold the smoke in their lungs for many seconds, more of these dangerous substances are consumed in one inhalation of marijuana than in one inhalation of tobacco. Nevertheless, even a heavy marijuana user smokes the equivalent of only a few cigarettes per day. That may explain why research has not found any evidence that marijuana-only smokers have an increased risk of developing lung cancer. Nevertheless, bronchial cell changes that appear to be precancerous have been seen in some people who smoke marijuana more than twice a day, which indicates that an increased risk of cancer among heavy users is definitely possible. More research, however, will be necessary to confirm this connection.

Does Marijuana Use Lead to Brain Damage?

The lungs are not the only place in the body that marijuana opponents say is at risk from marijuana use. They insist that marijuana use damages a person's brain. But like all issues associated with marijuana use, not everyone agrees.

A research study from the 1970s found structural changes in several brain regions in two rhesus monkeys that had been intentionally exposed to high doses of THC. Because these changes primarily involved the hippocampus, this finding suggested that brain damage (problems with learning and memory) in human marijuana users might be possible. Other studies on mice and rats found similar brain changes. Like many studies on marijuana's effects, however, all of these animal studies required exceptionally large doses of THC to produce observable changes to brain tissues, in some cases up to two hundred times the typical dose used by humans.

Several years later in another study, rhesus monkeys were exposed through face-mask inhalation to marijuana smoke that was equal to four to five joints per day for one year. When the monkeys were analyzed seven months later, the scientists found no changes in the hippocampus structure, cell size, cell number, or nerve connections, suggesting that even heavy marijuana use may not lead to irreversible changes in the hippocampus part of the brain. Because of research like this repudiating earlier reports of brain damage, the 1999 IOM report on medical marijuana concluded, "Earlier studies purporting [claiming] to show structural changes in the brains of heavy marijuana users have not been replicated with more sophisticated techniques."[4]

Despite this conclusion, opponents of marijuana insist that the research is not complete and that further studies will turn up evidence that marijuana use leads to brain damage. Thus studies continue to explore the effect of marijuana on brain functioning with ever-increasing scientific reliability. These latest studies have found that even though marijuana intoxication does not impair the brain's ability to retrieve information learned previously, it can, particularly when high doses are used, interfere with the ability to transfer new information into long-term memory. Therefore, most researchers conclude that marijuana can temporarily impair some memory functions, but that it does not cause permanent brain damage.

Does Marijuana Affect Male Fertility?

For many years scientists have known that in men, marijuana use also causes reduced fertility. A 2000 study conducted by scientists from the University of Buffalo found definite evidence that marijuana use has caused infertility in some men. This research proved that cannabinoids, both the body's natural cannabinoids and THC from marijuana, can prevent sperm from functioning normally. High concentrations of cannabinoids, for instance, can cause sperm to be less effective at fertilizing eggs. This fact led scientists to conclude that heavy marijuana users may jeopardize their fertility. How often this happens is still unknown, but the lead scientist in the University of Buffalo study stated, "The increased load of cannabinoids in people who abuse marijuana could flood the natural cannabinoid-signal systems in reproductive organs and adversely impact fertility. This possibility may explain observations made over the past 30 to 40 years that marijuana smoke drastically reduces sperm production in males."[5]

Does Marijuana Use Make People Unmotivated?

Marijuana is also sometimes said to make users passive, apathetic, unproductive, and unable or unwilling to fulfill their responsibilities. This combination of traits is called the amotivational syndrome.

The thought that marijuana causes amotivational syndrome in users first appeared during the late 1960s, as marijuana use was increasing among American youth. Whether or not marijuana makes people less motivated, though, is difficult to test and prove. For example, it is difficult to tell whether an unmotivated person became that way because of marijuana use or if that person was unmotivated for other reasons before ever trying marijuana. In efforts to better understand this issue, researchers conducted several large-scale studies of high school and college students. One study of college students found that marijuana users actually had higher grades than nonusers and that both groups were equally likely to successfully complete their educations. Other studies, these conducted in high schools, found little difference in grade-point averages between marijuana users and nonusers, except that one study found lower grades among students who used marijuana every day. That study's authors felt, however, that it was possible, based on profiles of the students, that the poor grades and marijuana use were part of a bigger set of social and emotional problems.

Besides studies comparing marijuana users and nonusers, considerable laboratory research has been directed at finding a link between marijuana use and amotivational syndrome. Most of these studies found that marijuana did not have a significant impact on motivation or learning and work performance. Such results have led researchers to suspect that people with low motivation from nondrug reasons—perhaps because they live with depression, illness, or poverty—are

420!

If there is truly such a thing as the marijuana culture, then its national holiday is April 20, or 4/20. For many years, marijuana users have used the number 420 as a symbol for their drug, and all around the world they have developed a tradition of smoking marijuana at 4:20 P.M. on 4/20. Furthermore, many pro-marijuana organizations hold rallies and lectures on April 20 each year.

There are several theories to explain the origin of 420 as a symbol of the marijuana culture. One theory says that 420 is a police code for marijuana use in some towns. Another theory says it represents the 420 chemical components supposedly found in marijuana. Others believe that a group of students met regularly after school and their meeting time, 4:20, became a symbol of marijuana smoking that somehow spread.

Whatever its origin, for many years 420 was a secret symbol understood only by members of the marijuana culture. Its symbolic meaning eventually leaked out into mainstream society, however, and it has since become commercialized, showing up on clothing, bumper stickers, and other merchandise.

more likely to use drugs, including marijuana. The 1999 IOM report on medical uses for marijuana supported this view, citing statistical evidence suggesting that people with preexisting low motivation levels are more likely to use alcohol and other drugs. The IOM report added that there is no evidence linking low motivation to marijuana use, stating: "When heavy marijuana use accompanies these symptoms [of low motivation], the drug is often cited as the cause, but no convincing data demonstrate a causal relationship between marijuana smoking and these behavioral characteristics."[6]

Currently available evidence strongly suggests that the health and social risks posed by marijuana are less than previously believed. Nevertheless considerable disagreement remains about whether or not marijuana and the existence of a marijuana culture are harmful.

 **Chapter 3**

Illegal Almost Everywhere

M arijuana is now illegal in most countries of the world. In the United States it is illegal to use, possess, grow, or sell marijuana in about three-quarters of the states. Many people ignore these laws, however; in 2000 an average of one marijuana smoker was arrested every forty-five seconds in America.

Recently, though, the illegal status of marijuana has come under ever-increasing criticism. This is due largely to a growing belief that outlawing marijuana, a drug many experts say is less harmful than alcohol or tobacco, has been an entirely unsuccessful and exceedingly expensive experiment.

Before Marijuana Was Illegal

In the United States, marijuana and other substances derived from the cannabis plant were first made illegal in 1937, but the story leading up to the various cannabis laws goes back to the turn of the twentieth century. In 1900 between 2 and 5 percent of the U.S. population was addicted to morphine, a drug that was the primary ingredient in numerous unregulated medications known as patent medicines. These medicines promised to cure just about every ailment from headaches to indigestion. Because of the strong pain-killing ability of morphine, the medications seemed to work. When the pain associated with disease or injury began to come back, an individual had only to go to the local store and buy another bottle of the patent medicine. Morphine is a highly addictive drug, however, so it was not long before people were buying their patent medicines frequently, and not necessarily because they were still in pain; instead, they bought the medicine to avoid the agony of withdrawal.

Patent medicines from the early twentieth century contained morphine, a highly addictive drug.

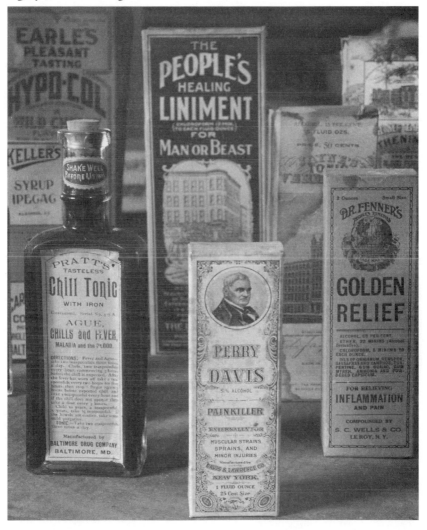

The federal government, alarmed at the growing number of unintentionally addicted citizens, responded in 1906 with the Pure Food and Drug Act. This law created the U.S. government's Food and Drug Administration (FDA). The FDA had the task of approving all foods and drugs meant for human consumption before they could be sold. The very first job of the FDA was to remove medicines containing morphine and other opium derivatives from the open market and make them available only by a doctor's prescription. Ultimately, the FDA's actions reduced the number of customers so much that the patent medicine manufacturers went out of business.

The Harrison Act of 1914

The Pure Food and Drug Act of 1906, which was not a criminal law, was extremely effective and reduced the level of addiction more than any of the many criminal drug laws enacted since. One such law, the Harrison Act, enacted in 1914, represented the first time drug use had ever been defined as a crime. This law applied only to derivatives of the drug opium (including morphine) and to derivatives of the coca plant (including cocaine). Although marijuana was not specifically covered by the Harrison Act, this unusual law is important in the history of marijuana illegality because it set the pattern, or precedent, for the federal drug legislation that followed.

The Harrison Act was unusual in that it was actually a *tax* law, and for the next fifty years American drug laws followed this model, indirectly making the use of certain pain medications a criminal act. The law taxed the nonmedical use of drugs like morphine and cocaine, strong painkillers to which up to 5 percent of the American population was addicted in 1900. The tax for nonmedical use of these drugs was far more than the cost of morphine or cocaine. People who used the drugs without paying the tax were subject to criminal prosecution.

Widespread Illegality

The Harrison Act paved the way for the national prohibition of cannabis. Between 1914 and 1937, twenty-seven different states made marijuana illegal. The states that passed these laws fell into two groups. The first states to pass marijuana laws were in the western part of the country. These states had recently experienced a large immigration of Mexican citizens, who had come north from their country in search of better economic conditions. They were mostly farmworkers, and some of them brought marijuana with them. Most of the non-Hispanic people in the western part of the United States mistrusted the new immigrants and knew nothing about marijuana. Consequently the first anti-marijuana laws were more of an expression of hostility toward the newly arrived Mexican community than opposition to the marijuana some of them used.

A second group of states that enacted criminal laws against the use of marijuana were in the northeastern part of the country. In these states there were few Mexicans, but northeastern residents had heard about the influx of Mexican immigrants out west and about the drug marijuana. These states had just begun to get the morphine addiction problem under control and feared that addicts, cut off from morphine, would substitute some other drug that was not yet controlled. In the absence of any research or medical information, marijuana seemed like a possible candidate for this substitution. So even though marijuana use was virtually unknown in the Northeast at that time, these states also outlawed it.

The Marihuana Tax Act

The law that made nonmedical use of marijuana (spelled *marihuana* in 1937) illegal was called the Marihuana Tax Act and was passed by Congress in 1937. How that law came to pass is a curious chapter in American lawmaking.

Whenever Congress considers a proposal for a new law, a congressional committee holds hearings to determine the facts surrounding the proposed law. Typically, these hearings require testimony from experts on all sides of the question, and it usually takes at least a few weeks to thoroughly examine all aspects of the proposed new law. Hearings on the new marijuana law, however, lasted only three days, and less than two hours of that time was devoted to testimony. Years later, when professors Richard Bonnie and Charles Whitebread were doing research for their book about the history of the marijuana laws, they were surprised to discover how little discussion took place in Congress before the new marijuana law was passed. They report:

When we asked at the Library of Congress for a copy of the hearings, to the shock of the Library of Congress, none could be found. . . . It took them four months to finally honor our request because the hearings were so brief that the volume had slid down inside the side shelf of the bookcase and was so thin it had slid right down to the bottom inside the bookshelf. That's how brief they were. They had to break the bookshelf open because it had slid down inside.[7]

Only a few people testified during that brief 1937 hearing. The first speaker was Harry Anslinger, the newly named commissioner of the Federal Bureau of Narcotics. Anslinger gave a very short testimony based on hearsay and unproven reports, which he summed up with the words, "Marihuana is an addictive drug, which produces in its users insanity, criminality, and death."[8]

Since outlawing marijuana would make all cannabis cultivation illegal, Congress also wanted to hear testimony from representatives of the rope, paint, and birdseed industries that used hemp for their products. Representatives from the rope and paint industries testified that they could use other raw materials in place of hemp. The representative of the birdseed industry, however, said no other seeds produced the glossy feathers that hemp seed did and they wanted to keep using hemp seed. As a result of that testimony, birdseed companies later received an exemption from the Marihuana Tax Act. They were allowed to use imported hemp seeds that have been treated so they do not sprout. That exemption remains in effect today.

Following testimony from Anslinger and representatives of the hemp industries, the congressional committee heard from the medical community. The first medical testimony came from James C. Munch, a pharmacology researcher at Temple University who studied the effects of drugs. Munch testified that he had injected into the brains of three hundred living dogs what he claimed was the active ingredient in cannabis, and that two of those dogs had died.

Researchers today argue that this was highly questionable science. The standard way scientists confirm new research is to publish the results of an experiment in a scientific journal and have those results independently reproduced by a number of other scientists. Munch's experiments with dogs and marijuana were never published, and no other scientist ever reproduced his results. Further, the true active ingredient in cannabis was not even identified until after World War

The Father of Marijuana Prohibition

When Harry J. Anslinger became the commissioner of the Bureau of Narcotics, he was already known for his very strong feelings about drug abuse. While the alcohol Prohibition Act was still in effect during the 1930s, for example, he criticized the law as being lenient; it penalized only people who sold, manufactured, and transported liquor, not people who bought and used it. Anslinger felt that the law should be changed so that buyers and consumers of liquor would also be punished, and he proposed harsh punishments to force the

Commissioner of the Bureau of Narcotics, Harry J. Anslinger, reports to a Senate Judiciary Subcommittee about drug use.

public to obey the liquor laws. He thought that a first-time conviction for buying alcohol deserved a jail term of not less than six months and a fine of not less than $1,000. He felt a second violation deserved imprisonment for two to five years and a fine of $5,000 to $50,000. Although his philosophy of punishing consumers of alcohol was not shared by most of Congress, he did manage to influence the lawmakers in that direction when it came to other substances, including marijuana.

The United States was suffering through the Great Depression when Anslinger became commissioner of the Bureau of Narcotics in 1930. It was a difficult time to get funding for any kind of project, even for law enforcement. To convince Congress to grant the bureau more funds, the commissioner had to prove there was a dangerous new drug threatening the country, one that required immediate federal attention and more money for the Bureau of Narcotics. He believed that dangerous new drug was marijuana.

Anslinger knew the power of public opinion, and he decided to use it. Under his guidance the bureau produced frightening stories about the evils of marijuana. These tales appeared in virtually every newspaper and publication. Lurid posters went up on billboards, in government offices, and on public transportation. And movies like *Reefer Madness* amplified the fear of marijuana that was growing in America. Although Anslinger, through his vast media campaign, almost single-handedly created the idea of a "marijuana problem" in the United States, much of what he did was the result of a sincere conviction that marijuana posed a danger to the country.

II in a laboratory in Holland. In 1937, however, no one else had done any research on marijuana. Thus, no one on the committee objected to Munch's testimony, and his statements were accepted as fact.

Following Munch, William C. Woodward, who was both a lawyer and a doctor, testified. Woodward was the top legal adviser for the American Medical Association (AMA), the organization that represents physicians in the United States. Testifying on behalf of the AMA, Woodward noted that the AMA did not consider Munch's research conclusive. Further, he said that the AMA had no other evidence of the harmfulness of marijuana. Woodward summed up his testimony with the words, "The American Medical Association knows of no evidence that marihuana is a dangerous drug."[9]

Films like Reefer Madness *and other media campaigns were used by the government to warn of the evils of marijuana.*

Politics Get in the Way

When the hearing ended, the committee shared what it had learned with the rest of the members of Congress, a common practice used before voting on a new law. Theoretically this is a good system, but sometimes political motivations prevent it from working the way it is intended to.

In 1937 Democratic President Franklin D. Roosevelt was in the middle of a successful push to get Congress to pass the huge package of economic and social reform legislation that came to be known as the New Deal. The overwhelmingly Democratic Congress was helping the president by attempting to discredit all opposition to New Deal legislation. The AMA, however, felt that the New Deal was bad for the medical profession and opposed most of the new legislation. Since the AMA constantly opposed the New Deal from 1932 to 1937, the Democrats who made up most of the marijuana hearing committee treated the AMA as their political enemy. This became obvious during the hearings. Following Woodward's statement that the AMA had found no evidence of marijuana's harmfulness, one of the New Deal congressmen went so far as to say, "Doctor, if you want to advise us on legislation, you ought to come here with some constructive proposals . . . rather than trying to throw obstacles in the way of something that the federal government is trying to do."[10]

So despite the AMA's opposition, the Marihuana Tax bill passed from the committee to the floor of Congress for debate and voting. The debate in the House of Representatives lasted only a few minutes. Only one pertinent question was asked from the floor: Did anyone talk to the AMA and get their opinion? Representative Carl Vinson, one of the New Deal Democrats who supported the marijuana bill, answered the question. Getting both the name of the AMA representative and the facts wrong in order to push the new law through, Vinson said, "Their Doctor Wharton gave this measure his full support . . . [as well as] the approval [of] the American Medical Association."[11]

Thus, the bill passed and went to the Senate, where it passed without debate. President Roosevelt immediately signed the bill into law, making marijuana essentially illegal in the United States.

Soon after the passage of the Marihuana Tax Act, Commissioner Anslinger appointed James C. Munch, the researcher who had injected marijuana into dog brains, to be the Federal Bureau of Narcotics' expert on marijuana. He held that position until 1962.

A Temporary Comeback for Hemp

In 1942, only five years after the Marihuana Tax Act outlawed all cultivation of cannabis, the United States was embroiled in World War II and found itself cut off from Asian sources of cheap hemp fiber. The country's warships needed a lot of hemp for rope, however, so the Marihuana Tax Act of 1937 was ignored while the federal government went into the business of growing hemp on large farms throughout the Midwest and the South.

Hemp cultivation ceased again when the war ended, but the results of that large-scale cultivation can still be seen in the extensive amount of wild hemp, called ditchweed, that reappears each summer throughout the Midwest. Although this ditchweed contains very little THC, various government and police agencies go to great trouble and expense to remove it every year.

The "Insane Killer" Drug

At the congressional committee hearing in 1937, Harry Anslinger, the commissioner of the Bureau of Narcotics, had said that marijuana causes, among other things, insanity. He was not just making this up. In fact, at that time there had been several well-publicized murder trials where the defendants' sole defense had been not guilty by reason of insanity due to having used marijuana prior to the commission of the crime.

To make the "innocent by reason of insanity" defense work, a defense lawyer must produce an expert witness who will testify that the defendant was truly insane, even if temporarily. During the 1930s and '40s when scientific research on marijuana was virtually nonexistent, there was only one witness in the country who could be called on to testify about the effects of marijuana. It was Munch, Anslinger's own marijuana expert who claimed to have injected the drug into dogs.

The most famous of the "defense by reason of insanity from marijuana" trials involved two women who had robbed and killed a bus driver, claiming that they committed the crime because they had gone temporarily insane after smoking marijuana. During the trial Munch justified his expert status by testifying that not only had he conducted the experiments on dogs and testified before Congress about it, but that he had tried the drug himself and it had made him temporarily insane. In this high-profile trial, he testified that after smoking two puffs of marijuana, he hallucinated that he had become a bat and flown around the room for fifteen minutes, ending up at the bottom of a giant inkwell.

During World War II, the need for stronger rope made from hemp fiber caused the federal government to ignore the Marihuana Tax Act of 1937.

Following Munch's sensational testimony, one of the defendants took the stand. She claimed that while she was under the influence of marijuana, she imagined that she grew vampirish fangs that dripped with blood. These testimonies convinced the jury that marijuana causes temporary insanity.

In the 1950s, the idea of marijuana use causing criminal insanity became a popular theme in pulp books.

In another murder trial during the same period, the defendant did not even claim to use the drug. He declared that there had been a bag of marijuana in the room and it had put out "homicidal vibrations" that made him kill dogs, cats, and ultimately two police officers. In the years immediately following the passage of the Marihuana Tax Act, where the marijuana defense was used, the defendants in those and other murder trials were all found innocent by reason of insanity.

Meanwhile, Anslinger was beginning to develop doubts that marijuana was the culprit in the murder cases, and he was bothered by the successful marijuana insanity defenses. He wrote to Munch and told him that if he did not stop testifying for the defense, he would be fired as the official marijuana expert of the Federal Bureau of Narcotics. The pharmacologist stopped testifying, and since there were no other marijuana "experts" around at the time, the "insanity by marijuana" defenses ended. By then, though, marijuana had become known as a drug that turned people into insane killers.

The Boggs Act of 1951

By 1950 the notion that marijuana was an addictive drug that caused insanity, criminality, and death was no longer accepted by many people. In the years since the marijuana hysteria of the 1930s, and despite the fact that the drug was illegal, marijuana use had continued to spread. As a result, more people witnessed its effects firsthand, and few believed the stories about insanity, criminality, and addiction. However, there was a growing sense in the United States that drug use among teenagers was increasing. Congress responded by introducing a new law, the Boggs Act, which carried much harsher penalties for marijuana use.

To pass a new law with harsher penalties, it was necessary to demonstrate that marijuana, if not the cause of insanity, criminality, and addiction, was nevertheless dangerous. As before, a congressional committee heard testimony. First a doctor who ran a government narcotics rehabilitation clinic in Kentucky testified that the medical community knew that marijuana was not an addictive drug and that it did not produce insanity, criminality, or death. The next witness, Commissioner Anslinger, reversed his earlier position, the one he expressed in his 1937 testimony, and agreed that marijuana was not addictive and did not produce insanity or death. Instead, he said, marijuana use is the first step to heroin addiction. That statement introduced the world to the idea that marijuana was the "gateway" to heroin, meaning that using marijuana makes the user more likely to use heroin, a highly addictive drug. In addition to introducing the concept of marijuana as a gateway drug, this represented the first time that it had been categorized with more dangerous drugs.

The Boggs Act had one more reason compelling Congress to vote for it. In 1951 the Cold War was in full swing, and many Americans feared that communist spies and infiltrators were everywhere. Newspapers published hundreds of articles asserting that enemies of the United States were trying to break down the moral fiber of the country's youth. The articles claimed that one way the country's enemies were supposedly doing this was by getting America's youth so hooked on drugs they would be incapable of defending their country should the need arise. Suddenly increasing the penalties for using or selling all nonmedical drugs sounded like a patriotic duty. The Boggs Act passed easily.

Ultimately, the Boggs Act had international consequences. World War II was over and the United States was the most economically and militarily powerful country in the world. Consequently, American laws influenced the laws of other countries. During the 1950s a flurry of new international agreements and laws in almost every country in the world were passed with little reason other than the Americans were doing it. These agreements, influenced by America's Boggs Act, led to outlawing nonmedical use of drugs, including marijuana, in most countries.

The Daniel Act of 1956

By 1956 the United States was responding with shock and anger to a new awareness of organized crime organizations like the Mafia. And Americans were learning for the first time that much of the huge profits going into the pockets of these criminal organizations came from the sale of illegal drugs.

Vito Genovese (in handcuffs) leaves court to begin a fifteen-year prison sentence. Genovese was the head of a large Mafia drug ring.

Congress and most state governments responded to the booming illegal drug business by further increasing the penalties for sale and possession of all drugs. One federal law, the Daniel Act of 1956, greatly increased the penalties of the Boggs Act by requiring the courts to give much longer sentences for drug crimes. The Daniel

Act included marijuana because people still feared it was the "gateway" to drugs like heroin and cocaine.

Many states followed the Daniel Act with their own versions, and like the new federal law, these provided harsher penalties than previous laws. Many states passed their own laws making possession of any drug the most heavily penalized crime in the state. Virginia's law, for example, required a mandatory minimum sentence of twenty years without possibility of parole, probation, or suspension of sentence for anyone found guilty of possessing any drug for nonmedical use.

The Dangerous Substances Act of 1969

Despite these new harsher laws, the illegal drug business continued to grow. In response, still another new federal law, the Dangerous Substances Act, was passed in 1969. This law took all the drugs known at that time (except alcohol and tobacco) and divided them into groups, or "schedules," based on what the government believed to be their medical value and potential for abuse. (It was also about this time that the government stopped calling all illegal drugs narcotics. This represented an official recognition that *narcotic* was the medical term for a drug that stops pain or puts people to sleep, a description that did not include many of the drugs being used in nonmedical ways.)

According to the Dangerous Substances Act, which has been modified over the years but is still largely in effect today, the most dangerous drugs are placed in schedules 1, 2, or 3. Schedule 1 drugs are those defined as having little or no legitimate medical use and a high potential for abuse; marijuana, hashish, LSD, and heroin were placed in this group. Schedule 2 drugs are those with accepted but limited medical value and a high potential for abuse, like cocaine, barbiturates, and amphetamines. Schedule 3 drugs are those with high medical value and a high potential for abuse, like morphine and codeine. The Dangerous Substances Act also provides penalties for illegal use, manufacture, and sale of the various drugs.

The Dangerous Substances Act of 1969 was the first federal drug law that had the benefit of some good new scientific research. It was also the first time an American law lowered most of the penalties for nonmedical use of drugs instead of raising them.

Recent Trends in Marijuana Laws

In the years immediately following the Dangerous Substances Act, the national attitude toward marijuana softened and penalties actually declined in many states; by 1980 eleven states had decriminalized possession of small amounts of cannabis for personal use. Declining penalties were accompanied by a decline in the number of people using the drug, a fact that challenged the popular belief that lesser penalties lead to greater use. In 1984 marijuana use (including both infrequent and frequent users) was 26.3 percent nationwide. In the eleven states that had decriminalized marijuana, it was almost the same, 27.3 percent. By 1988, after two decades of decreasing penalties and decriminalization in eleven states, the percentages of users had dropped to 15.4 nationwide and 16.1 in the states that had decriminalized marijuana. Instead of use climbing with lesser penalties, it had been cut almost in half.

As more legislators saw the significance of the statistics, some began to look favorably on decriminalization of marijuana use, meaning that individuals would no longer be arrested for possession of small amounts of cannabis. As of mid-2001 twelve states (Alaska, California, Colorado, Maine, Minnesota, Mississippi, Nebraska, Nevada, New York, North Carolina, Ohio, and Oregon) had decriminalized possession of small amounts of marijuana, and six others (Florida, Massachusetts, New Jersey, Texas, West Virginia, and Wisconsin) were poised to do the same. In many of those states, there is a small fine (up to $100) for possession, the result of a federal government requirement for minimum punishment standards.

International laws are changing, too, as the decriminalization movement grows around the world following the success of a Netherlands program that since 1976 has essentially allowed the personal use of cannabis. Following the adoption of the new policy toward marijuana use, the Netherlands saw a 40 percent decrease in marijuana use and an even larger drop in heroin addiction. These results led many other European countries, Canada, Australia, New

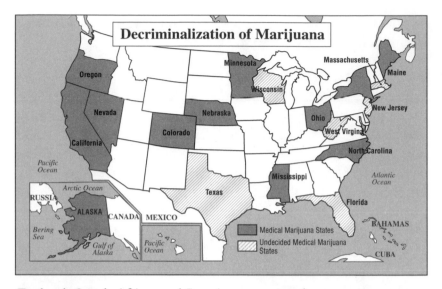

Zealand, South Africa, and Jamaica, among others, to pass or consider decriminalization laws.

Even as marijuana laws are changing in the United States and elsewhere, the drug remains illegal almost everywhere. And as long as marijuana remains illegal, some people will continue to press for laws that legalize and regulate its use.

 **Chapter 4**

The Responses to Illegal Marijuana Use

The popularity of marijuana makes its illegality a highly scrutinized and controversial topic. Even though it is the third most frequently used nonmedical drug after alcohol and tobacco and the most popular illegal drug in the world, it is also the subject of extensive efforts by law enforcement agencies to stop its importation, cultivation, transportation, sale, and use. Further, preventing people, especially young people, from using marijuana is the subject of numerous educational and treatment programs. Even so, widespread use of marijuana continues in the United States, leading some people to contend that the nation's marijuana laws should be changed.

Prohibition Again?

From 1919 to 1933, the United States undertook an experiment to stop the manufacture, transportation, and sale of all alcoholic beverages. The result was a set of laws known as Prohibition. Anslinger spoke about how he thought Prohibition should have punished the users of alcohol, an oversight that he intended not to repeat in the Marihuana Tax Act of 1937. In fact, the thinking and social concerns that led to alcohol prohibition strongly influenced the formation of America's early marijuana laws, and because of the

At a speakeasy, patrons buy illegal alcohol during Prohibition.

similarities, many people have called the illegality of cannabis "marijuana prohibition."

Today alcohol prohibition is generally viewed as a total failure. Prohibition not only failed to prevent alcohol consumption, but making the alcohol business illegal put it in the control of criminals who used increasingly violent means to control the market. Alcohol prohibition created a huge illegal business with extensive smuggling and secret domestic manufacturing operations. Illegality increased the prices of alcohol and the huge profits that resulted made alcohol smugglers and dealers very wealthy. The dealers and smugglers, in turn, commonly used their riches to bribe police and government officials into ignoring their illegal activities.

Other negative consequences of alcohol prohibition also appeared. Since hard liquor was more profitable to smuggle and manufacture, beer and wine almost disappeared and more people began to consume stronger alcoholic beverages. Organized crime, for the first time ever, became a fact of life in America. Further, to combat the resulting crime wave, the government created the largest police force that had ever existed in the United States, which led to more frequent violent encounters with criminals. All the while, to the government's astonishment, illegal alcohol sales continued to increase. Finally, after more than a decade of Prohibition, the government decided to repeal the laws and once again allow people to sell alcohol legally and to pay taxes on its sales.

Alcohol prohibition created a criminal empire, lost huge amounts of tax revenues, caused many deaths in the battles for control of the illegal business, led to the corruption of many police and politicians, and failed to achieve its goal of reducing alcohol consumption. Marijuana prohibition exhibits the same characteristics with one major difference: alcohol prohibition did not attempt to punish the users of the illegal substance.

Is Marijuana Prohibition Failing, Too?

Based on many government statistics and scores of studies, marijuana prohibition is even less successful and far more costly than alcohol prohibition was. First, assuming that the purpose of marijuana prohibition is to stop people from using marijuana, so far it has not succeeded. Marijuana has been illegal in the United States since 1937, yet marijuana use is at an all-time high and growing. Very few Americans had even heard of marijuana in 1937, but in 2001 nearly 70 million Americans had used it. During the 1980s the U.S. government declared an official "war on drugs," a government program aimed at reducing and even eliminating drug use in

America. Yet the federal government's Drug Enforcement Agency (DEA) reported that marijuana was more available in 2000 than it was in 1980.

In addition, many critics of marijuana prohibition contend that the cost to the criminal justice system has been staggering. Arrest rates are so high for marijuana and other drug offenses that prison officials sometimes are forced to release violent criminals early to make room for more drug offenders. And the ever-rising cost of the war against drugs drains funds from other social programs. For these reasons some people believe that marijuana prohibition has been more harmful to society than marijuana use.

A number of government and private studies and research reports have also arrived at this conclusion. Typical of these is a comprehensive, long-term study conducted by the Kaiser Permanente medical group that concluded no link exists between regular marijuana smoking and increased health problems. The report emphasizes that marijuana prohibition actually poses the most significant health hazard to the user and strongly suggests that "medical guidelines regarding [marijuana's] prudent use . . . be established, akin to the commonsense guidelines that apply to alcohol use." [12]

Marijuana Prohibition and Teen Marijuana Use

Government efforts to reduce marijuana use have focused, among other areas, on reducing teen use. Many studies, however, show that marijuana prohibition seems to have had exactly the opposite effect on cannabis use by teenagers.

Since marijuana prohibition began in 1937, marijuana use by teens has skyrocketed. In 1937 only 0.4 percent of all Americans under the age of twenty-one had ever smoked marijuana. By 1979, after forty-two years of heavy penalties for breaking the marijuana laws, that figure had jumped to 51 percent. This increase does not necessarily prove that marijuana prohibition actually caused more people under the age of twenty-one to use the drug, but it does illustrate that teen use increased dramatically despite the fact that marijuana use was against the law.

Opponents of marijuana legalization say the fact that prohibition does not seem to be working is no reason to legalize the drug. If

A young woman passes a pipe to someone at a 1960's love-in.

marijuana were legalized, they argue, teen use would simply increase. One federally funded study looked at this question by studying high school students' attitudes about drugs in states where decriminalization had occurred. Over a five-year period from 1975 to 1980, the researchers found that "decriminalization has had virtually no effect either on the marijuana use or on related attitudes and beliefs about marijuana use among American young people."[13]

With only one such study conducted in the United States, it is necessary to look elsewhere for additional evidence of how teen marijuana use changes when the drug is decriminalized. Studies published by governments in places where marijuana use has been decriminalized, including the Netherlands and two of Australia's eight territories, indicate that the rates of marijuana use across all age groups has not substantially changed after decriminalization.

Many people are baffled by the way marijuana prohibition has, for the most part, produced the opposite of the desired effects, particularly when it comes to curtailing use by young people. By prohibiting marijuana, the government expected that it would make the drug less available—but according to every report that has come out in the last two decades, this is obviously not the case. The federally funded Monitoring the Future survey, for example, found that in 1995 teenagers in many areas of the United States considered marijuana easier to obtain than beer. According to the report, "Every year, about 85 percent of the nation's high school seniors report that marijuana is 'fairly easy' or 'very easy' to obtain." [14]

In addition, the fact that using marijuana is against the law does not appear to be the primary factor in most teenagers' decision to use or not to use marijuana, much like the illegality of underage drinking seems to do little to deter underage drinking. In fact, a 1995 series of national public opinion surveys about marijuana found that "non-users were much more likely to mention 'not interested' than 'fear of legal reprisals' as the primary reason why they did not use marijuana." [15]

Further, the drug's illegality also sometimes works the opposite way for many teens, and the illegality of marijuana can actually increase the attractiveness of the drug. Best-selling natural health author Andrew Weil, M.D., wrote in 1993, "Because drugs are so surrounded by taboos, they invite rebellious behavior. . . . Unfortunately, our society's attempt to control drug-taking by making some substances illegal plays into the hands of rebellious children." [16]

Weil's statement was echoed by the Netherlands Institute of Mental Health and Addiction when that agency explained why marijuana use was decriminalized in Holland. The institute stated that to prevent alcohol and drug abuse, these substances must be "stripped of their taboo image and of the sensational and emotional tone of voice that did in fact act as an attraction." [17]

Marijuana Arrest Rates

Reducing the number of youthful marijuana users is just one goal of marijuana prohibition; the larger goal is to reduce the number of marijuana users of all ages. This goal is further from being achieved today than it was when the Marihuana Tax Act of 1937 was enacted. Despite more than half a century of anti-marijuana laws, despite the tens of billions of dollars spent on enforcing those laws, and despite the presence of drug education programs in schools, arrests for marijuana use are at an all-time high and still climbing.

The total number of annual marijuana arrests rose steadily during the 1960s and '70s, and then leveled off and even dropped during the '80s. Beginning in 1992, however, arrests for marijuana began climbing sharply again, a trend that has continued to the present time. Public records from the U.S. Justice Department's Bureau of Justice Statistics (BJS) show that there have been more than seven hundred thousand marijuana arrests every year since 1996, the highest numbers in history. Of these arrests, almost 90 percent are for possession rather than trafficking or selling.

Also, according to BJS figures, in 1998 the average number of marijuana offenders in jail or prison, not counting those awaiting trial, was close to sixty thousand. About thirty-seven thousand of those were convicted of possession. The BJS estimates that the direct costs to American taxpayers for maintaining this population of marijuana prisoners in federal and state prisons and local jails is about $1.2 billion per year.

The Financial Cost of Marijuana Prohibition

Exact figures on how much the government spends specifically on marijuana prohibition are not available, but it is possible to make a conservative estimate based on the available figures for fighting all illegal drugs. The Department of Justice (DOJ) reports that the federal expenditure for all categories of drug law enforcement (investigating and arresting people and seizing drugs) is well over $15 billion a year. In addition, state and local governments spend an additional $16 billion per year enforcing drug laws. Adding these two figures means that the total cost of enforcing the drug laws in America is at least $31 billion per year. Based on DOJ estimates that between 25 and 40 percent of all drug arrests are for marijuana, the cost to American taxpayers of enforcing just the marijuana laws is between $7.8 billion and $12.4 billion each year.

These huge sums of public money must be diverted from other causes, causes like education and fighting violent crime. Further, each of the more than half a million arrests made each year in the United States for violating marijuana laws, even the most trivial arrest, removes at least one or two police officers from crime fighting for several hours while they complete the paperwork and process the defendant. This adds up to millions of man-hours per year that could be used for fighting more serious crime.

Police officers arrest a protester at a demonstration in support of legalizing marijuana.

Recognizing that this is a problem, some state governments have tried to reduce these costs. In 1976 California passed the Moscone Act, a marijuana decriminalization law that reduced the penalty for possession of small amounts of the drug to a citation and a small fine. As a result of the Moscone Act, police in California no longer arrest people for small amounts of marijuana, and courts and jails are no longer clogged with marijuana users. Further, according to a 1988 report, "California has saved an average of $95.8 million annually during the ten years since the Moscone Act was passed."[18] An in-depth study is needed, however, to calculate the true cost of marijuana prohibition.

Marijuana and the "War on Drugs"

Despite the success in California and other states, the federal government has not shown much interest in backing down from its opposition to decriminalizing marijuana. Instead, the government has remained committed to its "war on drugs," a term that describes the immense effort to reduce drug availability and use in the U.S.

The marijuana part of the government's war on drugs has several components. The most obvious one is the constant effort of local police and DEA agents to catch, arrest, and punish users (except in the states where it has been decriminalized) and dealers. But there are other components in the war on drugs that often go unseen by the general public, components that require immense amounts of manpower, equipment, and money. These are interdiction (stopping the importing of cannabis products), eradication (stopping the growing of cannabis within U.S. borders), and education (stopping the use of marijuana).

Interdiction

For many years the United States has concentrated much of its military, technological, and law enforcement might into stopping marijuana and other drugs from entering the country. The amounts of marijuana seized by authorities during this time are huge. In 1997, for example, along the country's southwest border, a record 593 tons of marijuana were intercepted. Even so, the DEA estimates that despite all the government's massive interdiction efforts, only 15 percent of the marijuana coming into the United States gets stopped.

According to the DEA, drug-trafficking organizations based in Mexico supply most of the foreign marijuana available in the United States. However, countries in South America (primarily Colombia) and Asia (including Cambodia, Thailand, India, and Pakistan) also cultivate and ship marijuana to the United States.

Foreign marijuana bound for U.S. markets must be smuggled into the country. Smugglers resort to a great variety of methods of getting the bulky drug across the borders, using everything from trucks to ships and aircraft. Even though the government seizes many tons every year, most experts agree, and the statistics back them, that it is virtually impossible to stop this flow of marijuana into the country. This is a troubling fact to the many people involved in the war on drugs.

Eradication

Besides curbing the flow of marijuana into the United States, officials are also focusing on cultivation of the drug within the country. Beginning in the 1970s, cannabis cultivation within the borders of the United States began to blossom. This was primarily the result of two factors. First, increased interdiction pressure on drug smugglers has decreased the availability of imported (smuggled) marijuana. The second reason is that marijuana's tremendous profit potential makes people willing to take the risk of growing cannabis in or close to their homes. The wholesale value of American-grown marijuana (its value to the farmers who grow it), by the DOJ's most conservative estimates, has exceeded $15 billion every year since 1995. And on the retail market, domestic marijuana is worth more than $25 billion. This makes marijuana the fourth largest cash crop in the country, with only corn, soybeans, and hay ranking as more profitable. According to 1998 DEA and state police statistics, marijuana cultivation produces more money than any other crop in Alabama, California, Colorado, Hawaii, Kentucky, Maine, Rhode Island, Tennessee, Virginia, and West Virginia, and ranks as one of the top five cash crops in twenty-nine other states. In fact, the government estimates that at least a quarter of the marijuana consumed by Americans is grown within the country's borders.

An Eradication Story from California

Sometimes eradication efforts are successful. During the summer of 2000, an eleven-week sweep of California marijuana growing areas produced a record haul. During that operation, called Campaign Against Marijuana Planting (CAMP), a total of 345,207 marijuana plants were seized at large-scale growing operations around the state. The raids resulted in the arrests of fifty-seven people, and officials estimated the cash value of the seized marijuana at $1.3 billion.

Successful raids like these are not easy. Eradicating the big bushy plants, even ones that are growing right out in the open, is more difficult than it might seem. To make the dark green marijuana plants less visible to spotters in planes and helicopters, growers usually spread the plants around instead of planting them in rows like conventional crops. When task force agents are successful at spotting marijuana from the air, the hard work starts. The sites are rarely accessible from public roads, so the raids are often carried out by helicopter. In some cases agents are lowered to the ground in slings because the remote ravines and hillsides where the plants grow are too rocky, steep, or thickly forested for helicopters to land. Once on the ground, the agents cut the plants and load them into a sling to be hauled up into the helicopter and transported away for destruction.

A helicopter hauls away $15 million worth of marijuana plants that were growing in a California national forest.

It takes a lot of cannabis plants to produce that much marijuana, and the DEA first noticed the growing amount of domestic cultivation during the late 1970s. The U.S. government, specifically the DEA, responded in 1979 by starting the Domestic Cannabis Eradication/Suppression Program (DCE/SP). This program initially included two multiagency operations, one in Hawaii and the other in California, whose goal was to eradicate marijuana cultivation in those states. Gradually other states discovered that they, too, had marijuana growing within their borders and began participating in the program. By 1982 twenty-five states were involved in the DCE/SP, and by 1985 all fifty states had joined it.

DCE/SP's eradication program uses advanced technology, including military aircraft, remote infrared sensing devices, and satellites to find outdoor marijuana crops, and thermal imaging systems for finding indoor growing operations. In addition, the DCE/SP sometimes uses herbicidal eradication, similar to the defoliation program used during the Vietnam War. Herbicidal eradication relies on controversial plant poisons, and most states still don't allow their use. Oklahoma was the first state to use herbicidal marijuana eradication, and Hawaii, South Dakota, and Indiana have joined the list.

Because of pressure from the DCE/SP, many marijuana growers have been forced to move their operations indoors, where their crops are better hidden from helicopters and satellites. At first this seemed like a victory for the DCE/SP, but it soon became apparent that this was not the case at all. Indoor cultivation, as both the DEA and growers soon discovered, provides a controlled environment that favors the production of higher potency grades of marijuana. Indoor cultivation also permits year-round production and can be carried out everywhere from closets, garages, attics, and basements to elaborate, specially constructed greenhouses. Furthermore, growth rates of indoor cannabis plants can be more precisely controlled and enhanced by special fertilizers, plant hormones, steroids, insecticides, and genetic engineering, advantages that are nearly impossible outdoors.

Indoor cultivation is not completely immune to detection by law enforcement agencies, however. The special high-intensity lights used

Marijuana plants are grown indoors in efforts to escape detection from the U.S. Drug Enforcement Agency.

by growers to take the place of sunlight consume large amounts of electricity, so buildings with unexplained high electrical bills are likely to draw the attention of the DEA. Government agents then used thermal sensing technology to identify garages and closets in private homes that are too hot due to the presence of the high-intensity lights. In 2001, however, the U.S. Supreme Court, in a ruling on an indoor marijuana cultivation case, voted that using thermal-sensing technology to investigate private homes is an unconstitutional invasion of privacy and could no longer be used as a basis for obtaining a search warrant (permission for the police to search a home).

The government's eradication program requires considerable manpower, aircraft, and other equipment, all of which are expensive. To justify requests for more funding, the eradication program's administrators must present evidence of large marijuana seizures to prove that the program is working. Critics of the program discovered that the government was counting ditchweed in their marijuana seizure figures. This practice, say the critics, creates the impression that the program is far more successful than it actually is. Ditchweed, the wild cannabis that grows in fields and ditches, mostly throughout the Midwest, has very low THC content and no value as marijuana. Critics say if ditchweed were removed from the government's eradication figures, the amount of destroyed marijuana would be so low that the program would be considered a failure.

Education

Many people, including some government and law enforcement officials, believe that interdiction and eradication efforts are having little success. Consequently, many feel that education programs may offer the best hope for reducing marijuana use.

The nation's major drug education program is known as D.A.R.E., an acronym for Drug Abuse Resistance Education. Former Los Angeles police chief Daryl Gates founded the first D.A.R.E. program during the late 1970s to teach children about the dangers of drugs. Since then it has expanded to become the federal government's favored drug education program. Today the national D.A.R.E. program receives about $600 million a year from federal, state, and local governments, and employs uniformed police officers, who go into schools to present the program.

At first, educators and parents welcomed a drug education program in schools. After years of unquestioning community acceptance, however, the D.A.R.E. program has recently found itself facing growing opposition from all sides. Numerous research and government agencies have issued scathing critiques of the program, accusing D.A.R.E. of having little or no impact and arguing that the approximately $600 million a year from federal, state, and local governments used to fund it might be better spent elsewhere. One government study reported that D.A.R.E. students were not less likely to use drugs than students not involved in the program. That report concluded, "D.A.R.E. could be taking the place of other, more beneficial drug use curricula that adolescents could be receiving."[19]

Further, in California, where the program began, researchers found that 40 percent of the students surveyed were "not at all" influenced by D.A.R.E. programs, and only 15 percent were influenced "a lot" or "completely." Nearly 70 percent described a "neutral to negative" feeling toward the D.A.R.E. officers.

Numbers and reports like these have caused parents, teachers, students, and government officials to become increasingly dissatisfied with the D.A.R.E. program. Consequently, D.A.R.E. officials announced in 2001 that the program was being completely redesigned.

Treatment Programs

One reason government officials spend so much time and money on marijuana interdiction and eradication is that they believe marijuana is addictive. Even though marijuana use has not been associated with the life-wrecking effects of alcoholism or health-damaging effects of nicotine addiction, some marijuana users do have to seek treatment to help them stop using the drug. A small percentage of marijuana smokers (anywhere from 1 to 5 percent) develop a dependency on the drug and feel that they cannot function without it or stop using it. Some of these people seek treatment on their own. Others are ordered by employers or a court to attend a treatment program.

One of the most common treatment programs is Marijuana Anonymous (MA), an organization that helps users learn to live without the drug. Based on a twelve-step program pioneered by Alcoholics Anonymous, MA meetings bring together people with similar experiences who feel they are either emotionally or psychologically addicted to marijuana. MA meetings provide a sense of camaraderie that allows members to feel comfortable admitting that using marijuana causes problems in their lives.

Programs like this are becoming increasingly popular because many people now believe that treating marijuana users is preferable to putting them in jail. The newest and boldest effort to put marijuana and other drug users into treatment programs instead of prison began in July 2001 in California when the state's Proposition 36 took effect. This new law directs judges to require treatment instead of jail for most nonviolent drug users on their first and second offense. Previously, treatment had been an option only if offenders pleaded guilty and a judge approved. Under the new law, approximately thirty-seven thousand offenders in California will be eligible for treatment the first year. Officials estimate that this will save the state about $250 million a year in prison costs. Courts, prosecutors, and police officials around the country are eagerly awaiting the results of this new law, which if it is successful may encourage similar laws in many other states.

Legalization?

Some people feel that requiring treatment programs instead of jail time still does not solve the problems associated with marijuana prohibition. These people, marijuana smokers and not, want to see marijuana legalized.

The reasons for legalization are as varied as the people who support it. Some want marijuana to be legalized for sick patients who can benefit from its usage. Others want it to be legalized so that more hemp products, which have proven environmental and industrial benefits, can be produced. Still others want it to be legalized to cut off criminal profits and to create tax revenues for the state and federal governments. And then there are those who want it legalized so they can use it when they want to without fear of legal consequences.

One outspoken advocate for legalizing marijuana and other drugs is James Gray, a superior court judge in California. In 2001 Gray said;

> Based upon my background as a former federal prosecutor in Los Angeles, a criminal defense attorney in the Navy and as a trial judge in Orange County[,] California[,] since 1983, I believe we must change . . . our laws of drug prohibition and develop a policy based upon truthful drug education, drug treatment, deprofitization of these often dangerous drugs, and, most importantly, individual responsibility. . . . [T]o me it makes as much sense to put people like the actor Robert Downey, Jr. in jail for drug abuse as it would have to put [former first lady] Betty Ford in jail for her alcohol abuse. And even if people somehow disagree with that view, from my experience on the bench, we have proved to any reasonable person's satisfaction that this approach [putting drug users in jail] simply doesn't work. [20]

A Quaker Speaks Out on the Drug War

The Quaker faith, also known as the Society of Friends, is one of America's original religious groups. In a February, 1996, article titled "Getting Off Drugs: The Legalization Option," that appeared in the Friends Journal, *a leading Quaker spokesman, Walter Wink, made a strong case for changing the way the United States deals with drug use.*

The drug war is over, and we [the United States] lost. We merely repeated the mistake of Prohibition. The harder we tried to stamp out this evil, the more lucrative we made it, and the more it spread. An evil cannot be eradicated by making it more profitable. . . . Drug laws have also fostered drug-related murders and an estimated 40 percent of all property crime in the United States. The greatest beneficiaries of the drug laws are drug traffickers, who benefit from the inflated prices that the drug war creates. Rather than collecting taxes on the sale of drugs, governments at all levels expend billions in what amounts to a subsidy of organized criminals. . . .

The uproar about drugs is itself odd. Illicit drugs are, on the whole, far less dangerous than the legal drugs that many more people consume. Alcohol is associated with 40 percent of all suicide attempts, 40 percent of all traffic deaths, 54 percent of all violent crimes, and 10 percent of all work-related injuries. Nicotine, the most addictive drug of all, has transformed lung cancer from a medical curiosity to a common disease that now accounts for 3 million deaths a year worldwide. . . . We must be honest about these facts, because much of the hysteria about illegal drugs has been based on misinformation. . . .

It is safe to say as we approach the end of the eighth decade of federal control of inebriating drugs that the experiment has been a dismal and costly failure. . . . Already 95 percent of our adult population is using drugs, and the vast majority do so responsibly. Most people who would misuse drugs are already doing so. . . . No one wants to live in a country overrun with drugs, but we already do.

Although considerable disagreement about how the American government should go about legalizing marijuana remains, most supporters agree that the way alcohol is regulated and taxed in the United States provides a workable model. Judge Gray offers this view of what a marijuana legalization law would look like:

Marijuana, defined as cannabis with a THC content greater than 0.3 percent, may be purchased by anyone who is 21 years of age or older at a package store which sells only this product, and may be purchased, possessed and used by that same person without criminal or civil penalty. Reasonable taxes will be accessed for this sale, and the revenues raised will be used exclusively for drug and alcohol education and treatment. Furnishing marijuana to anyone under the age of 21 years of age, driving a motor vehicle under the influence of marijuana, etc. are prohibited by this initiative. [21]

Since the 1970s the United States has spent tens of billions of dollars in what most deem to be a largely unsuccessful effort to stop the flow of marijuana into the country. Hundreds of thousands of men and women have been imprisoned for marijuana offenses as the government continues to pour billions of dollars into enforcement, interdiction, eradication, and education campaigns of questionable effectiveness. In spite of this, most studies indicate that marijuana prohibition has failed to stop marijuana from entering the country, from being grown in the country, and from being used by ever-increasing numbers of people. Nevertheless, the efforts continue as the government searches for effective ways to control people's use of marijuana.

 **Chapter 5**

The Debate over Medical Marijuana

The mere mention of the phrase *medical marijuana* is enough to get at least two groups of people agitated. There are those who believe marijuana should be accessible to patients whose doctors have recommended cannabis to improve their medical condition. These people are angry that the federal government and many states continue to insist that marijuana does not have legitimate medical value. On the other hand, opponents of medical marijuana fear that the issue is just the first step toward legalizing cannabis (and maybe other outlawed drugs).

Between 1996 and 2001, several developments occurred that have repeatedly brought the medical cannabis debate to the attention of the American public. First, beginning in 1996, voters in many states passed laws permitting access to marijuana for patients who have a doctor's statement verifying medical need. Second, places where people with doctors' statements could purchase the drug legally, called medical marijuana buyers' clubs, began to appear in the states where the new laws had been passed, creating the controversial situation of public marijuana sales. Third, in 1997 Barry McCaffrey, the federal government's highest drug law enforcement official, ordered an analysis of all the research ever done on marijuana. The analysis was conducted by a team of top scientists, took two years to complete,

Demonstrators march to protest a federal lawsuit that opposes distributing cannabis for medical purposes.

and resulted in a report that said cannabis does indeed have medical value, is not a gateway drug, and, while not harmless, is less harmful than alcohol and tobacco. Finally, one of the medical marijuana buyers' clubs fought the federal government's prohibition of their operation all the way to the U.S. Supreme Court and lost.

The Medical Uses of Cannabis

For a long time patients, doctors, and scientists have attributed a variety of therapeutic functions to marijuana and other THC-containing preparations. One of the most remarkable things about cannabis, say medical marijuana advocates, is that it can alleviate a wide spectrum of symptoms at one time with minimal side effects. Most notably, cannabis has been credited with reducing nausea and pain while improving appetite and a variety of movement problems.

Treating all of these symptoms at once without toxic side effects has made marijuana the treatment of choice for many HIV/AIDS and cancer patients as well as people suffering from a number of other diseases. Many HIV/AIDS patients claim marijuana gives them relief from pain, nausea, and wasting disease (loss of body mass). And thousands of cancer patients have claimed that marijuana is the best way to alleviate the loss of appetite, nausea, and vomiting that often accompany chemotherapy, which is used to treat many kinds of cancer.

Patients are not the only ones claiming marijuana has medicinal value, however. Recent research has found that some of the cannabinoids in marijuana have the capability to help protect nerves from further damage following trauma and neurological disease. And scientists contend that there is considerable evidence that using marijuana can also improve the limitations in joint movement and muscle function associated with multiple sclerosis and spinal cord injury.

Despite these claims, opponents often assert that the medical marijuana movement is nothing more than the first step toward legalization of all drugs. They also contend that even when marijuana does have some medical value, there are other drugs—legal drugs—that do the job better.

Both sides in the medical marijuana argument do agree, however, that there are some concerns to using marijuana as a medicine. First is the method of ingestion: inhaling smoke from burning plant material has definite health hazards. Second, the therapeutic values of cannabis, including pain relief, control of nausea, and appetite stimulation, can all be achieved by other drugs that are legal. Third, the euphoric effect of marijuana is an undesirable side effect for many patients.

As in most aspects of the marijuana debate, this agreement quickly turns into disagreement. Doctors and their patients who use marijuana say that the three concerns should actually be viewed as advantages. First, inhalation allows very accurate control of the dosage by the patient: smoking gives the therapeutic effect within seconds; the effects would not be felt for thirty minutes or more if the drug were taken orally (as a pill, for example), which increases the chances of under- or overdosing. Second, marijuana is the only known drug that produces multiple desired effects in a single drug, thus eliminating the need for patients to take a variety of drugs that also have a variety of side effects. Third, the euphoric effect of cannabis can reduce anxiety and calm patients.

In the medical marijuana debate, such totally opposite views are typical. Often what one side sees as a problem the other sees as an advantage. Perhaps the only clear fact about medical cannabis is that marijuana is still illegal at the federal level. Given that, the Institute of Medicine (IOM) set about to determine the truths about medical marijuana.

Investigating the Medical Value of Marijuana

In 1997 the director of the White House Office of National Drug Control Policy (ONDCP), General Barry McCaffrey, faced a big public relations problem. Even though McCaffrey, several former presidents, and many others lobbied against medical marijuana initiatives in California and Arizona, the citizens of those states voted to legalize medical marijuana. McCaffrey stuck to his conviction that marijuana was not medicine and vowed that the federal government would prosecute patients and doctors who broke federal marijuana laws.

In response to the new laws, McCaffrey began an effort to defeat medical marijuana legislation in other states. Despite his efforts, seven other states went ahead and legalized medical marijuana. In looking for a way to slow the building momentum of the medical marijuana movement, McCaffrey commissioned a report from the IOM, which he felt sure would support his position.

The U.S. National Academy of Sciences, the federal sponsor of much of the scientific research that occurs in the United States, created the IOM in 1970 to provide politically independent scientific advice to the government. McCaffrey's ONDCP paid the IOM $896,000 to create a committee of unbiased scientists to evaluate all the research on marijuana and produce a comprehensive report on its dangers and medical value. The committee released the study, titled *Marijuana and Medicine: Assessing the Science Base*, in 1999.

McCaffrey must have been shocked after reading the report. The IOM study, the most comprehensive government study of marijuana to date, took an opposing view of almost every one of McCaffrey's own beliefs about the drug. The study reported, for example, that the committee found no proof that marijuana use leads to use of

Informally known as the nation's drug czar, Barry McCaffrey was the director of the White House Office of National Drug Control Policy, stepping down from office in January 2001.

harder drugs. It declared marijuana's addictiveness to be much less than legal drugs like alcohol and tobacco and of little consequence. It found that almost every harmful side effect that had ever been attributed to marijuana had no basis in scientific fact, and it acknowledged that marijuana did, in fact, have legitimate medical value.

Disappointed, McCaffrey and the ONDCP chose to ignore the IOM's conclusions and publicly criticized and contradicted the report. Until he resigned in 2001, McCaffrey continued to insist that marijuana leads to the use of harder drugs, is extremely addictive, and has no medical usefulness.

Among those criticized by McCaffrey was neurobiologist Janet Joy, the scientist heading the IOM committee. She publicly expressed embarrassment at McCaffrey's public attack on the report and defended it, saying the IOM report reflected the most rigorous academic standards. She told reporters that the committee's scientists and physicians, among the best in the country, had thoroughly analyzed more than two thousand scientific studies on marijuana over a two-year period. She also stated that the IOM report was based solely on medical evidence that measured the ways people are affected by cannabis, evidence that has been duplicated and confirmed numerous times by other researchers.

Most Americans agreed with Joy and the conclusions of the IOM report. In a nationwide Gallup poll conducted in 1999 after the report was published, 73 percent favored making marijuana legal for doctors to prescribe to suffering patients.

The Institute of Medicine Report

The 1999 IOM report was what scientists call a meta-analysis, meaning experts study all the research on a particular issue (medical marijuana in this case) to determine the facts and make conclusions. The IOM meta-analysis targeted very specific issues, including what medical conditions have been successfully treated by marijuana, what advantages marijuana has over legal medicines, how dangerous marijuana's side effects are, and if allowing the use of marijuana for medical purposes would promote nonmedical uses of the drug.

Protesters rally in San Francisco, California, to oppose a federal lawsuit that would close buyers' clubs distributing medical marijuana.

After studying the research on these issues, the IOM committee came to some conclusions. First, they said that marijuana was helpful, particularly for AIDS and cancer patients. The introduction to the IOM report states:

> There are some limited circumstances in which we recommend smoking marijuana for medical uses. . . . The accumulated data indicate a potential therapeutic value for cannabinoid drugs, particularly for symptoms such as pain relief, control of nausea and vomiting, and appetite stimulation. . . . For patients such as those with AIDS or who are undergoing chemotherapy and who suffer simultaneously from severe pain, nausea, and appetite loss, cannabinoid drugs might offer broad-spectrum relief not found in any other single medication. [22]

That last point illustrates one of medical marijuana's chief advantages over other drugs used to treat AIDS and cancer patients. Instead of taking a number of different drugs, most with significant side effects, a patient can decrease a variety of symptoms with just marijuana, which has relatively minor side effects. The IOM report confirmed that there is no single drug currently available that can do the several things that marijuana does.

Addressing the possibility of a patient becoming addicted to marijuana, the IOM report found that according to all evidence, dependence among marijuana users is rare. Further, the researchers said the dependence and withdrawal symptoms associated with smoked marijuana are "mild and subtle compared with the profound physical syndrome of alcohol or heroin withdrawal." [23]

The IOM report also found no evidence that marijuana is a gateway drug likely to lead to using other drugs. And the report responded to the concern that allowing the medical use of marijuana might increase its use among the general population, in particular, among young people, stating, "No evidence suggests that the use of opiates or cocaine for medical purposes has increased the perception that their illicit use is safe or acceptable. . . . [T]here is little evidence that decriminalization of marijuana use necessarily leads to a substantial increase in marijuana use." [24] Finally, the IOM report explained that the danger of marijuana's side effects is actually less than the medically accepted levels of side effects associated with many legal drugs.

The one harmful aspect of using marijuana for medical purposes, said the IOM report, is the fact that currently the most effective way to take the drug is by smoking it, which may lead to lung and respiratory problems. The report added, however, that the respiratory cancers found in many chronic tobacco smokers have not been found in people who smoke marijuana daily (if they do not use tobacco). And although the researchers expressed a desire for an effective alternate means of delivering marijuana to patients, the report determined that currently existing alternatives (including Marinol, a pill of synthetic THC available by prescription since the 1980s) are not nearly as effective as the smoked form.

The IOM report concluded by stating that marijuana offers substantial therapeutic advantages. Nevertheless, the IOM committee felt that more research is needed to confirm the scope of the drug's usefulness and its side effects and to discover alternative delivery methods that are as effective as but less harmful than smoking.

Medical Marijuana Research

Research into medical applications of marijuana is made all the more difficult by the fact that all forms of cannabis remain in the schedule 1 category, which makes it almost impossible for scientists to obtain marijuana of consistent potency needed for studies. Often current marijuana laws make it very difficult for scientists at universities and pharmaceutical companies to get permission to do cannabis research at all. And if they succeed in getting permission to do cannabis research, it is very difficult for them to obtain the drug legally. Furthermore, confiscated marijuana that researchers obtain from law enforcement sources (a common source of marijuana used in cannabis research programs) varies greatly in potency and is sometimes tainted by other drugs, pesticides, and other impurities. Nevertheless, scientists have continued to do what research they can.

One important discovery took place during the 1990s when scientists found naturally occurring cannabinoid molecules in mammals, including humans, and cannabinoid receptors in the brain and the body. Researchers identified about half a dozen of these cannabinoids in the human body, which made them want to look more closely at the hundreds of cannabinoids found in marijuana. Scientists want to learn more about why the body has these natural relatives of the cannabinoids in marijuana. Further, pharmaceutical companies want to know if the cannabinoids in marijuana can help the body's own cannabinoids for some therapeutic purposes. Recent research has found, for instance, evidence that some cannabinoids, both the body's own and those found in marijuana, can control some movement disorders, such as Parkinson's disease and Tourette's syndrome, and researchers have also found indications

Marijuana for Brain Cancer?

Malignant glioma is a fairly common, especially aggressive, and often fatal form of brain cancer. Existing treatments for this disease have a low success rate, but recent research on rats indicates that cannabinoids from marijuana may be able to stop the disease in humans. In the research, which was performed in Spain and reported in the March 2000 issue of the scientific journal *Nature Medicine,* malignant brain tumors either disappeared or were reduced in two-thirds of cancerous rats injected with cannabinoids. The cannabinoid treatments caused no damage to healthy cells.

The lead researcher on the project—Manuel Guzman, Ph. D., a professor of biochemistry in Madrid (Spain)—is concerned that the debate over medical marijuana use will hinder future testing of this treatment in humans. In Liza Jane Maltin's February 2000 online article "Marijuana's Active Ingredient Targets Deadly Brain Cancer," Guzman is quoted as saying, "If these compounds were present in pine leaves or lettuce, then most likely things would be different. But they are present in marijuana, so it's controversial, which is nonsense. Hospitalized patients are given morphine and other drugs, but for some reason, it's considered immoral to give them cannabis."

Daniele Piomelli, Ph. D., a professor of pharmacology at the University of California, Irvine, agrees, saying in an editorial that accompanied the journal article, "Placing restrictions on clinical use and testing of marijuana-based therapies is not only silly, it can be criminal. When patients are dying, there should be no consideration to such matters. . . . I believe it would be ethically acceptable to offer [cannabinoids] to patients, especially in light of the fact that the toxicity is likely to be very, very small."

that cannabinoids can play a role in controlling some forms of high blood pressure.

Cannabinoid research is also looking at the problems associated with medical marijuana use. One involves separating the medical aspects of cannabis from the aspects that make a patient high; the euphoric effect that so many recreational marijuana users seek is viewed as an adverse side effect in medical applications. Another major challenge for medical marijuana research is finding ways of administering the active ingredients (THC and other cannabinoids) without requiring the patient to smoke it. Besides introducing its own health problems, smoking is an issue in medical marijuana because many patients do not smoke or are so sick they cannot tolerate smoking. Thus, some pharmaceutical companies are developing alternative ways to administer THC. These include an aerosol inhaler much like those used to dispense asthma medication, an under-the-tongue spray, and a transdermal skin patch containing the medication in a small bandage that allows the drug to be absorbed through the skin.

Doctors and Medical Marijuana

As the research continues, the doctors who would be affected by legalizing medical marijuana remain almost evenly divided on the topic. In April 2001, in response to a question about whether doctors should be able to prescribe marijuana legally as a medical treatment, 36 percent of the physicians surveyed thought they should, 38 percent thought they should not, and 26 percent were neutral.

In some cases the specialty of the doctor affected the position. For instance, the survey found that obstetricians, gynecologists, and internists were more likely to support medical marijuana than other specialists. The survey team speculated that because doctors in those two specialties are more likely to see cancer patients, they may be more aware of marijuana's potential for managing pain and the side effects of chemotherapy and therefore more receptive to using marijuana for medical therapy.

Whether they support medical marijuana use or not, many doctors resent the intrusion of nonmedically trained politicians and law enforcement officials into the debate on medical marijuana. One of the most outspoken critics of the government's medical marijuana policy is Lester Grinspoon, M.D., an associate clinical professor of medicine at Harvard Medical School who has written two books on the medicinal use of marijuana and served as an official at NORML. After his son died from leukemia (a cancer of the blood system), Dr. Grinspoon became an avid medical marijuana activist, often recommending marijuana to his cancer and AIDS patients. Speaking about his firsthand experience with the medical use of marijuana, Grinspoon said:

Dr. Lester Grinspoon supports the use of medical marijuana to relieve the pain and nausea caused by AIDS and cancer treatments.

I had a son with leukemia, and I saw with my own eyes how helpful cannabis was in dealing with the nausea that he had with chemotherapy. The memory of him eating a submarine sandwich after chemotherapy—and keeping it down—is one I will never forget. . . . I know better than any federal official what's best for my patients and whether marijuana can help them. I'm not going to be told by those [federal officials] how to practice medicine.[25]

State and Federal Governments Disagree

Despite claims like Grinspoon's, the federal government decided to challenge the Oakland Cannabis Buyers' Cooperative, a large, highly visible nonprofit organization that provided medical marijuana to patients in northern California and was and still is legal under state law. In May 2001 the U.S. Supreme Court unanimously ruled in this case that since marijuana is classified as a schedule 1 drug (no medical value, high potential for abuse), it has no legal medical use and the Oakland Cannabis Buyers' Cooperative could not continue providing marijuana to patients. This was seen as a major defeat for those who want access to the drug to relieve the symptoms of HIV/AIDS, cancer, and other diseases.

The Oakland Cannabis Buyers' Cooperative

When California voters passed Proposition 215, the law officially known as the Compassionate Use Act of 1996, people with a doctor-certified need for medical marijuana were elated. But since it was still illegal to sell marijuana in the state, patients were faced with the problem of how to obtain the drug legally. The need was filled by a new phenomenon, medical cannabis buyers' clubs and cooperatives.

As suppliers of marijuana to medically approved buyers, these organizations were protected from prosecution by state law. The only problem was that their actions were still against federal laws. Eventually one of the first buyers' clubs, the Oakland Cannabis Buyers' Cooperative (OCBC), became the subject of a federal lawsuit, a case that went all the way to the U.S. Supreme Court. Following the Court's mid-2001 decision against them, however, the OCBC was no longer able to dispense marijuana to its members.

The mission statement of OCBC, as stated on the Oakland Cannabis Buyers' Cooperative website, www.rxcbc.org, says:

> The goal of the Oakland Cannabis Buyers' Cooperative (OCBC) is to provide seriously ill patients with a safe and reliable source of medical cannabis information and patient support. Our cooperative is open to all patients with a verifiable letter of recommendation for medical cannabis, used to alleviate or terminate the effects of their illnesses.

> Federal statutes currently prohibit the use of cannabis as medicine. However, scientific evidence, including anecdotal evidence, documents the relief that cannabis provides to many seriously ill patients. The cooperative is dedicated to reducing the harm these patients encounter due to the prohibition of cannabis.

Following the Supreme Court decision, Republican Congressman Bob Barr said:

> The unanimous vote in this case reflects the overwhelming evidence that marijuana has been appropriately and lawfully declared to be a dangerous, mind-altering substance that should not be legalized for whatever contrived reason. The true aim of those who support the so-called medical marijuana movement has been . . . the legalization of all drugs. Terminally ill patients have been used as pawns in a cynical political game designed to weaken society's opposition to drug abuse.[26]

The federal government's position, though, did not significantly affect the beliefs of state legislators, who are often more supportive of medical marijuana. In fact, within weeks of the U.S. Supreme Court's ruling, Colorado's legislature passed a new state constitutional amendment protecting medical marijuana users from state criminal penalties; the amendment followed eight other states that had, beginning with California in 1996, passed similar legislation. The new Colorado law, which allows legally registered patients to possess up to two ounces of marijuana and/or six marijuana plants, directly opposes the Supreme Court's ruling that people or organizations that grow or distribute marijuana may not use medical necessity as a defense from federal prosecution. Defiant in the face of the Supreme Court decision, Colorado's attorney general Ken Salazar announced that the Supreme Court's ruling did not invalidate Colorado's state law or prevent the medical use of marijuana in the state. California's attorney general Bill Lockyer agreed, saying, "It's unfortunate that the Supreme Court was unable to respect California's historic role as a . . . leader in the effort to help sick and dying residents who have no hope for relief other than through medical marijuana."[27]

Most legal experts feel that the Supreme Court decision does not prevent patients in states with medical marijuana laws from growing their own marijuana at home. But not all patients are able to do that, and they no longer have a source in the buyers' clubs. Since almost all arrests for use and possession of marijuana are done by state and local officials, the federal government is expected to confine enforcement efforts to shutting down medical marijuana distribution centers like the Oakland Cannabis Buyers' Cooperative, which triggered the Supreme Court case.

Although the immediate effect of the Supreme Court ruling was to stop the distribution of marijuana to patients in those states with medical marijuana laws, it may ultimately have another effect. Essentially the Supreme Court ruling said that as long as marijuana is classified as a schedule 1 drug, the only way to get it approved at the federal level for medical use would be for Congress to pass a new law reclassifying cannabis as a schedule 2 drug (limited medical value, high potential for abuse) or even schedule 3 (high medical value, high potential for abuse). As a result, following the Supreme Court decision, Democratic Congressman Barney Frank reintroduced legislation allowing certain patients to use marijuana for medical purposes and doctors to prescribe or recommend marijuana where permitted under state law. If that or similar legislation eventually passes, marijuana will be reclassified, paving the way for legalizing medical marijuana at the federal level.

Founder of the Oakland Cannabis Buyers' Cooperative, Jeff Jones (right), speaks with his lawyer after the Supreme Court rules marijuana illegal for medical uses.

Judges and Medical Marijuana

The justices of the Supreme Court notwithstanding, however, there is a growing trend among American judges to accept that medical use of marijuana has a place in American society. Most surprising among the many judges who have made public statements in favor of medical marijuana is Francis L. Young, a DEA administrative law judge. In 1988 Judge Young presided over a hearing in which several groups petitioned the DEA to have marijuana reclassified as a schedule 2 drug so it could be prescribed for medical needs. After considering all the testimony and exhibits, Judge Young wrote a report for the DEA stating that the court "accepted as fact" the medical value of cannabis. He listed numerous examples from individual doctors, hospitals, and patients demonstrating the medical uses of cannabis. Young concluded by saying that cannabis is "far safer than many foods we commonly consume . . . and in its natural form it is one of the safest therapeutically active substances known to man. By any measure of rational analysis marijuana can be safely used within a supervised routine of medical care."[28]

Young is not the only judge who thinks this. In doing research for his 2001 book on the failure of the war on drugs, California Superior Court Judge James P. Gray found many other judges willing to declare their support for medical marijuana. He himself is a staunch supporter of allowing medical uses of marijuana, and in a 2001 interview Judge Gray said:

> I have never used marijuana, or any of these other drugs either . . . and I have never smoked cigarettes. I believe marijuana is a carcinogenic [cancer causing], and does have other adverse effects upon the user. However, it is hard for me to be unduly hard upon marijuana users since I do drink alcohol, and believe that alcohol is potentially far more harmful to the user than marijuana, and the actions of people who have used alcohol are potentially far more harmful to other people.[29]

Despite such strong opinions by well-respected judges, the DEA has refused, without giving a reason, to reclassify cannabis. Immediately after Judge Young's report was made public, editorials began appearing in newspapers asking why the DEA was so intent on keeping marijuana illegal in the face of so much evidence that the drug's illegality was by far the biggest, most expensive, and most unsuccessful part of the war on drugs. Judge Gray offers an explanation in his book when he points out that since marijuana users make up the vast majority of all drug users, without them the "enemy" in the drug war would instantly shrink to a fraction of its current size. Then the numbers of drug users, contends Gray, would be too small to justify the tens of billions of dollars consumed by the DEA. Of course, he claims, the DEA *needs* to keep marijuana illegal. The DEA, however, continues to insist simply that marijuana is a dangerous drug.

In 2001 Canada passed a new law allowing patients access to medical marijuana. This new legislation, the first federal-level medical marijuana law in the world, also provides for a company to legally grow and distribute cannabis to approved patients. With medical marijuana now legal in Canada, pressure to change the cannabis laws is even greater in the United States. Nevertheless, medical marijuana, like everything else about the drug, remains a controversial topic in American politics.

Notes

Chapter 2: Is Marijuana Use Really Harmful?

1. Janet E. Joy, Stanley J. Watson Jr., and John A. Benson Jr., eds., *Marijuana and Medicine: Assessing the Science Base.* Institute of Medicine, Division of Neuroscience and Behavioral Health. Washington, D.C.: National Academy Press, 1999, p. 3.
2. Joy et al., *Marijuana and Medicine*, p. 90.
3. Joy et al., *Marijuana and Medicine*, p. 89.
4. Joy et al., *Marijuana and Medicine*, p. 106.
5. Kristin Leutwyler, "Marijuana Definitely Linked to Infertility," *Scientific American*, December 12, 2000. www.sciam.com/news/121200/2.html.
6. Joy et al., *Marijuana and Medicine*, p. 102.

Chapter 3: Illegal Almost Everywhere

7. Richard J. Bonnie and Charles H. Whitebread II, "The Forbidden Fruit and the Tree of Knowledge: An Inquiry into the Legal History of American Marijuana Prohibition," *Virginia Law Review* 56, no. 6, October 1970, p. 53.
8. Bonnie and Whitebread, "The Forbidden Fruit and the Tree of Knowledge," p. 53.
9. Bonnie and Whitebread, "The Forbidden Fruit and the Tree of Knowledge," p. 54.
10. Bonnie and Whitebread, "The Forbidden Fruit and the Tree of Knowledge," p. 54.
11. Bonnie and Whitebread, "The Forbidden Fruit and the Tree of Knowledge," p. 55.

Chapter 4: The Responses to Illegal Marijuana Use

12. Michael Polen et al., "Health Care Use by Frequent Marijuana Smokers Who Do Not Smoke Tobacco," *Western Journal of Medicine* 158, no. 6, June 1993, pp. 569ff.

13. Lloyd Johnston, Patrick O'Malley, and Jerald Bachman, "Marijuana Decriminalization: The Impact on Youth, 1975–1980," *Monitoring the Future Occasional Paper 13*. Ann Arbor, MI: Institute for Social Research, 1981, pp. 27ff.

14. Lloyd Johnston, Jerald Bachman, and Patrick O'Malley, *National Survey Results on Drug Use from the Monitoring the Future Study, 1975–1995*. Washington, DC: National Institute on Drug Abuse, 1996, p. 88.

15. Johnston et al., *National Survey Results on Drug Use*, p. 89.

16. Andrew Weil and W. Rosen, *From Chocolate to Morphine: Everything You Need to Know About Mind-Altering Drugs*. Boston: Houghton Mifflin, 1993, p. 98.

17. Trimbos-Instituut, *Education and Prevention Policy Alcohol and Drug Fact Sheet*. Utrecht: Netherlands Institute of Mental Health and Addiction, 1996, p. 2.

18. Michael Aldrich and Tod Mikuriya, "Savings in California Marijuana Law Enforcement Costs Attributable to the Moscone Act of 1976—A Summary," *Journal of Psychoactive Drugs* 20, no. 1, January–March 1988, p. 81.

19. S. Ennett et al., "How Effective Is Drug Abuse Resistance Education?: A Meta-Analysis of Project D.A.R.E. Outcome Evaluations," *American Journal of Public Health* 84, no. 9, September 1994, pp. 1394ff.

20. James P. Gray, Drugsense Chat transcript, Media Awareness Project website, June 3, 2001. www.mapinc.org/drugnews/v01.n1122.a06.html.

21. Gray, Drugsense Chat transcript.

Chapter 5: The Debate over Medical Marijuana

22. Joy et al., *Marijuana and Medicine*, p. 3ff.

23. Joy et al., *Marijuana and Medicine*, p. 89ff.

24. Joy et al., *Marijuana and Medicine*, p. 102ff.

25. Quoted in Beatrice Motamedi, "Mary Jane Medicine," *WebMD Medical News*, February 21, 2000. www.webmd.com.

26. Quoted in Sean Martin, "Drug Law Allows No Exceptions for Medical Use, Justices Say," *WebMD Medical News*, May 14, 2001. www.webmd.com.

27. Quoted in Larry Margasak, "Court Rules Against Marijuana Use," *WebMD Medical News,* May 15, 2001, www.webmd.com.
28. Judge Francis L. Young, "Marijuana Rescheduling Petition, Docket No. 86-22, Opinion and Recommended Ruling, Findings of Fact, Conclusions of Law and Decision of Administrative Law," September 6, 1988. www.calyx.net/olsen/ MEDICAL/YOUNG/young.html.
29. Gray, Drugsense Chat transcript.

Organizations
to Contact

Californians for Compassionate Use
www.marijuana.org

This is one of the leading organizations advocating legalization of marijuana for medical purposes.

Drug Enforcement Administration
DEA Information Office
2401 Jefferson Davis Highway
Alexandria, VA 22301
Website: www.dea.gov

This is the arm of the Department of Justice dedicated to drug law investigation and enforcement.

International Association for Cannabis as Medicine
Arnimstrasse 1A
50825 Cologne, Germany
Phone: 49-221-9543-9229
Website: www.acmed.org

This nonprofit organization provides information about medical cannabis to individuals, organizations, and governments all over the world.

International Cannabinoid Research Society
55 Elsom Pkwy
S. Burlington, VT 05403
Phone: 802-865-0970
Website: www.cannabinoidsociety.org

This nonprofit organization is dedicated to research in all fields relating to cannabinoids.

Marijuana Anonymous World Services
P.O. Box 2912
Van Nuys, CA 91404
Phone: 800-766-6779
Website: www.marijuana-anonymous.org

Based on the principles of Alcoholics Anonymous, provides help for marijuana users who want to stop using the drug.

Marijuana Policy Project
P.O. Box 77492
Capitol Hill, Washington, DC, 20013
Website: www.prr.org

This national organization (chapters in every state) is dedicated to minimizing the harm caused by marijuana laws.

National Organization for the Reform of Marijuana Laws (NORML)
1001 Connecticut Ave.NW, Suite 710
Washington, DC 20036
Phone: 202-483-5500
Website: www.norml.org

This is the national organization for the reform of marijuana laws.

Reality Check
P.O. Box 2345
Rockville, MD 20852
Phone: 800-767-0117
Website: www.health.org/reality

The U.S. Department of Health and Human Services runs this campaign to help parents and other adults help children to understand the issues around marijuana use.

National Institute on Drug Abuse
5600 Fisher's Lane
Rockville, MD 20867
301-443-1124
Website: www.nida.gov

This is the U.S. federal government's center for anti-drug information.

For Further Reading

Books

National Institute on Drug Abuse, *Marijuana: Facts Parents Need to Know*. Washington, DC: USGPO, 1995. This is information on marijuana presented by one of the central anti-drug agencies of the federal government.

Andrew Weil and W. Rosen, *From Chocolate to Morphine: Everything You Need to Know About Mind-Altering Drugs*. Boston: Houghton Mifflin, 1993. Written for nonscientists, this is fascinating and unbiased writing.

L. Zimmer and J Morgan, *Marijuana Myths, Marijuana Facts: A Review of the Scientific Evidence*. New York: Lindesmith Center, 1997. An objective and clear analysis of the facts about marijuana. The Lindesmith Center is a respectable organization that provides a library of unbiased material relating to the drug war.

Website

Schaffer Library (www.druglibrary.org/schaffer/hemp/medical/medical.htm). This website contains a wealth of information on medical marijuana.

Works Consulted

Books

Nelba Chavez and the Substance Abuse and Mental Health Services Administration, *Key Influences on Youth Drug Use Identified*. Washington, DC: Department of Health and Human Services, 2001. A statistical analysis of influences on young people leading to the use of drugs.

——, *Substance Abuse in Popular Movies and Music*. Washington, DC: White House Office of National Drug Control Policy, Department of Health and Human Services, 1999. A mostly scientific look at the topic.

James P. Gray, *Why Our Drug Laws Have Failed and What We Can Do About It: A Judicial Indictment of the War on Drugs*. Philadelphia: Temple University Press, 2001. A recent book that builds the most powerful attack on current drug laws yet.

Lester Grinspoon, *Marihuana Reconsidered*. Cambridge, MA: Harvard University Press, 1977. This marijuana expert, both a doctor and Harvard professor, reveals the misunderstandings behind marijuana prohibition in an intelligent manner.

Lester Grinspoon, and James B. Bakalar, *Marijuana: The Forbidden Medicine*. New Haven, CT: Yale University Press, 1993. This book takes up where Grinspoon's earlier book stopped and makes a strong case for medical marijuana.

Lloyd Johnston, Jerald Bachman, and Patrick O'Malley, *National Survey Results on Drug Use from the Monitoring the Future Study, 1975–1995*. Washington, DC: National Institute on Drug Abuse, 1996.

Janet E. Joy, Stanley J. Watson Jr., and John A. Benson Jr., eds, *Marijuana and Medicine: Assessing the Science Base*. Institute of Medicine, Division of Neuroscience and Behavioral Health. Washington,

DC: National Academy Press, 1999. This report is extremely useful, fact filled and quite definitive for anyone interested on how marijuana and medicine relate, but it is not easy to read unless you have a background in medicine and biochemistry.

Laura Murphy, *Marijuana Cannabinoids Neurobiology and Neurophysiology*. Boca Raton, FL: CRC Press, 1992. This volume is packed with heavy marijuana science.

Michael Starks, *Marijuana Chemistry, Genetics, Processing, and Potency*. New York: Ronin, 1990. This book presents the heavy science of marijuana.

Trimbos-Institute, *Education and Prevention Policy Alcohol and Drug Fact Sheet*. Utrecht: Netherlands Institute of Mental Health and addiction, 1996.

Periodicals

Michael Aldrich and Tod Mikuriya, "Savings in California Marijuana Law Enforcement Costs Attributable to the Moscone Act of 1976—A Summary," *Journal of Psychoactive Drugs* 20, no. 1, January–March 1988. A scientific article full of statistics and analysis of the first medical marijuana bill.

Richard J. Bonnie and Charles H. Whitebread II, "The Forbidden Fruit and the Tree of Knowledge: An Inquiry into the Legal History of American Marijuana Prohibition," *Virginia Law Review* 56, no. 6, October 1970. This is an unbiased and lengthy article written for law students about the history of the marijuana laws.

S. Ennett et al., "How Effective Is Drug Abuse Resistance Education?: A Meta Analysis of Project D.A.R.E. Outcome Evaluations," *American Journal of Public Health* 84, no. 9, September 1994. This article studies all the research on D.A.R.E. programs and draws conclusions.

Federal Bureau of Investigation, "Crime in the United States: 1997," FBI Division of Uniform Crime Reports. Washington, DC: U.S. Government Printing Office, 1998. A government report filled with statistics.

Wayne Hall and Nadia Solowij, "Adverse Effects of Cannabis," *Lancet* 352, 1998. This is a scientific analysis of every harmful effect ever attributed to marijuana.

Lloyd Johnston, Patrick O'Malley, and Jerald Bachman, "Marijuana Decriminalization: The Impact on Youth, 1975–1980," *Monitoring the Future Occasional Paper 13*. Ann Arbor, MI: Institute for Social Research, 1981. This is a dry but informative look at surveys and other metrics concerning marijuana and young people from the sociological angle.

Michael Polen et al., "Health Care Use by Freqent Marijuana Smokers Who Do Not Smoke Tobacco," *Western Journal of Medicine* 158, no. 6, June 1993.

Sean Reilly, "Senator's Letter to General Accounting Office Prompts Inquiry," *Mobile (Alabama) Register*, February 6, 2001. This article describes former anti-drug warrior Senator Sessions changing ideas about the drug war.

Chuck Thomas, "Marijuana Arrests and Incarceration in the United States," *Drug Policy Analysis Bulletin*, no. 7, June 1999. This very informative article presents a scientific look at police statistics.

Walter Wink, "Getting Off Drugs: The Legalization Option," *Friends Journal*, February 1996.

Internet Sources

David Barry, "Calif. Pot Busts Set Record—Authorities Seize $1.3 Billion Worth in Latest Campaign," All Points Bulletin website, October 24, 2000. www.apbnews.com/newscenter/breakingnews/2000/10/24/pot1024_01.html.

James R. Gray, Drugsense Chat transcript, Media Awareness Project website, June 3, 2001. www.mapinc.org/drugnews/v01.n1122.a06.html.

Kristin Leutwyler, "Marijuana Definitely Linked to Infertility," *Scientific American*, December 12, 2000. www.sciam.com/news/121200/2.html.

Liza Jane Maltin, "Marijuana's Active Ingredient Targets Deadly Brain Cancer," *WebMD Medical News*, February 28, 2000. www.webmd.com. This is an article written for a general audience about a new medical use for THC.

Larry Margasak, "Court Rules Against Marijuana Use," *WebMD Medical News*, May 15, 2001. www.webmd.com.

Sean Martin, "Drug Law Allows No Exceptions for Medical Use, Justices Say," *WebMD Medical News*, May 14, 2001. www.webmd.com.

Beatrice Motamedi, "Mary Jane Medicine," *WebMD Medical News,* February 21, 2000. www.webmd.com. This medically reviewed article gives a brief overview of medical marijuana written in layperson's terms.

Judge Francis L. Young, "Marijuana Rescheduling Petition, Docket No. 86-22, Opinion and Recommended Ruling, Findings of Fact, Conclusions of Law and Decision of Administrative Law," September 6, 1988. www.calyx.net/olsen/MEDICAL/YOUNG/young.html.

Website

Oakland Cannabis Buyers' Cooperative (www.rxcbc.org). Here is the story on the first legal medical marijuana source that was closed by the U.S. Supreme Court.

Index

Picture Credits

About the Author

William Goodwin is a writer and channel manager for an online health information service. He also works as a consultant and speaker. He has been a science teacher at the high school and middle school levels, where he also taught drug abuse prevention classes. He earned a BA from UCLA and did his graduate work in biochemistry and later in English at UCSB and UCSD.

1
2
3